LIGHT AND LOVE

Dianne Lotter

PublishAmerica
Baltimore

PublishAmerica has allowed this work to remain exactly as the author intended, verbatim, without editorial input.

Softcover 9781630042028
eBook 9781630046804
PUBLISHED BY PUBLISHAMERICA, LLLP
www.publishamerica.com
Baltimore

Printed in the United States of America

ACKNOWLEDGEMENTS

It is with the permission of Father Kieran Kavanaugh, OCD, that I use his translation of *"The Sayings of Light and Love"* of St. John of the Cross. These sayings are the backbone of my book, and I am deeply grateful to Father Kavanaugh.

From *God Speaks in the Night* translated by Kieran Kavanaugh. The text only is copyrighted © 1991 by Washington Province of Discalced Carmelites ICS Publications 2131 Lincoln Road, NE Washington, DC 20002-1199 U.S.A. www.icspublications.org

From *The Collected Works of St. John of the Cross,* translated by Kieran Kavanaugh and Otilio Rodriguez Copyright © 1964, 1979, 1991 by Washington Province of Discalced Carmelites ICS Publications 2131 Lincoln Road, N.E. Washington, DC 20002-1199 U.S.A. www.icspublications.org

FOREWORD

The following "Sayings of Light and Love" are taken from the book *The Collected Works of St. John of the Cross"* translated by Kieran Kavanaugh, O.C.D. and Otilio Rodriguez, O.C.D. I have chosen the sayings from p. 85 to p. 97. Father Kieran Kavanaugh, O.C.D. has given me permission to use some of these sayings in my book *"Light and Love"*. It is with great gratitude towards Father Kavanaugh that I proceed to publish my book.

A little about who St. John of the Cross is, taken from *God Speaks In The Night, the Life, Times and Teaching of St. John of the Cross. ICS Publications translated by Kieran Kavanaugh, O.C.D.* " This book helps us come into direct contact with the life of St. John of the Cross, highlighting his solitude, travel and religious formation. We see him, too, constructing monasteries, writing books and caring for the sick. St. John of the Cross is a saint, mystic, theologian, priest and poet, living in the 16th Century Spain. He was a contemplative in action and did not live in undisturbed solitude. He is one of the greatest Carmelite Saints."

Since I am a Secular Carmelite and have been for about 20 years, it was natural for me to read many writings of St. John of the Cross. For those of you who do not know what it means to be a Third Order Carmelite or Secular Carmelite as we are now called, think of it this way…the First Order Carmelites are Priests, the Second Order Carmelites are Brothers or Sisters (nuns), and the Third Order Carmelites, now called Secular Carmelites, are lay people like me. Being a Secular Carmelite is a lifetime commitment. As Carmelites, we say the Breviary or Divine Office daily, every day and night of our lives, and when we die we may be buried in the brown habit if we so choose. As a Carmelite, I am familiar with the readings of almost all of the Carmelite Saints, such as St. Teresa of Avila, St. Therese of Lisieux, and of course, St. John Cross and many others.

Saint Faustina is not a Carmelite, but a very well known Saint of our times. I have read her Diary about 20 times, and much of my thinking develops as a result of reading her book as well as reading the Carmelite Saints. One of the devotions she has made famous is "The Chaplet of Divine Mercy", which is what I talk about here in this book. For those of you who don't know St. Faustina, I will share some thoughts on who she is. I read her book *The Diary of St. Faustina, Divine Mercy In My Soul,* by Saint Maria Faustina Kowalski, by Marians of the Immaculate Conception, Stockbridge, Massachusetts, on an ongoing basis. Along with St. John of the Cross, St. Faustina has helped greatly to shape my present spirituality. Even thought I don't quote her throughout the book, I attribute many of my thoughts to my ongoing study of her life and her writings.

LIGHT AND LOVE

Introduction:

I am attempting something which seems impossible to me…I want to share my deep faith with the world. I am using "The Sayings of Light and Love" of St. John of the Cross as a structure upon which I hope to build my thoughts and meditations. I wish to intersperse many thoughts that come to me also from reading "The Diary of St. Faustina" and thoughts which strike me from the daily reading of the Divine Office. This is to admit that most of what I write is not mine. However, when I read the above mentioned books, I am filled with inspirational thoughts, and it is these thoughts that I wish to share with you. My days are filled with prayer, reading, and meditation, and it is at these times I am most urged to share. I admit that the numbers of the Sayings are not in any particular order.

#1. "Sayings of Light and Love"

"The Lord has always revealed to mortals the treasures of his wisdom and his spirit, but now that the face of evil bares itself more and more, so does the Lord bare his treasures more."

I can't help but think that there is more evil in the world now than ever before—more than in the time of St. John of the Cross. I feel moved to pray for all of the sinners in the world, for most of them do not give a thought about eternity. They only think of the here and now. They have no notion about the fact that someday they will be judged by their Creator. Some of these sinners parade their treasures as though they are the luckiest or best people on earth. What will be their thoughts on their deathbed, for all will certainly die?

When I pray the Chaplet of Divine Mercy, as taught by Sister—Saint Faustina, I pray for these sinners, who surround us and are found everywhere, that God will have mercy on them. I never know who I am praying for, or if they will be blessed enough to ask for God's mercy on their deathbed, but like St. Faustina, I pray for these unknown souls, and beg God to send down His mercy on them, especially at the time of their death.

#2. "O Lord, my God, who will seek you with simple and pure love, and not find that you are all one can desire, for you show yourself first and go out to meet those who seek you?"

My Lord, yes, You are all one can desire. Whoever desires You above all, possesses the greatest treasure there is upon this earth, …possesses the greatest joy and happiness that can be found. You not only go out to meet us who desire You, … You are the One who planted that desire in our soul, and for this we can be eternally grateful. In today's Office, we read, "The precepts of the Lord are right. They gladden the heart. The command of the Lord is clear, it gives light to our eyes.

The fear of the Lord is holy, abiding for ever. The desires of the Lord are truth and all of them just. They are more to be desired than gold, than the purest of gold, and sweeter are they than honey, than honey from the comb."1 It is hard to think of anything more beautiful, more enticing, than the precepts of the Lord. If you are one of these people, consider yourself to be most blessed, for there is no greater treasure on earth than the word of God. We seek God, but the truth is, He seeks us. If we find Him, we come to realize that He first sought us, and how blessed we are. He truly is all we can desire. There is nothing in this world that I desire more than my desire for God in my life. But who am I? I am only an ignorant and foolish person. How can I be so lucky, so blessed, as to realize that I have found the "pearl of great price"?

#16. "O sweetest love of God, so little known, whoever has found this rich mine is at rest!"

This saying brings with it such deep joy and peace that I can't begin to describe it. God is everywhere, although most people don't see His presence surrounding them. Once one's eyes are opened to seeing God everywhere and in everything, there is no more complaint of life's trials. We are all beset by trials, some more, some less. If we could only see that by accepting these trials graciously as coming from the hand of God for our benefit, the trials would lose their sting. Instead, we would recognize that God gives us the grace and strength to bear the trial, and He gives the joy which surrounds us as we pass through the trial.

I have experienced a great trial for the past five years. On looking back, I see myself as I struggled through it. It was the hardest in the beginning, because I didn't see God's hand in it. Once I came to understand that He would give me the strength to bear it, if all I did was to ask, then I managed to get through it somehow. I now realize that it was only with His grace, His presence in my life, and His strength, that I managed to get through it. Even today, though the trial has lessened somewhat, I see that the only path for me out of this dark forest, is to cling to God's hand. He will continue to lead me forward, and He will beckon me to advance through to what someday will be the light.

Yes, I believe I have found this rich mine, the sweetest love of God. I am so eager to show others this pathway through a forest of darkness. Yet I know that I can't. Only God can lead us through. Only by taking His hand, following His lead, can we find Him in our lives, in the midst of our dark trials. John Michael Talbot sings, "He who has God wants for nothing at all." I find this to be the absolute truth. In possessing God, there is nothing to distract us, nothing to entice us away from the good. There is nothing we want, nothing of value on this earth that can draw us away from this Great Good which is God. How many of us get lost in the tangle of earthly goods, the enticement of riches, or beauty or fame?

How many of us realize that we are not made for this earth but for heaven—a heaven which lasts for an eternity? And how often do we reflect on what eternity actually is? There is no simple word or group of words that can accurately describe eternity. It is beyond our comprehension. Sometimes I look out the window and see the leaves on all the trees in the whole world. Then I begin to imagine counting all the grains of sand, or all the drops of water, or all the snowflakes. My mind becomes boggled with the idea that this number doesn't even begin to match the number of years in eternity. Eternity is forever! Yet, how easily are we drawn to things which lessen our grip of ever being desirous of an eternity of bliss? How often are we stuck in the events of a day, or a week, or a year? What does all of this matter in the light of eternity?

When I hear this, that the love of God is so little known, it causes me great pain. I long to share with the rest of the world this sweetest love of God. I search for ways, but I don't know how. The only way I know of sharing my deep love for God is to write about it and then I come to realize that I can only do this with God's help. For who am I, this little unknown creature, looked down upon because I am so poor in material things? If only the world could know that I feel richer than any queen or princess, because what I do have is of great price. I have the peace and joy which the world would envy, if it knew. And where do I find this peace and joy? One place I find it is at Church, by attending Daily Mass. I also find it by doing little sacrifices for the love of God throughout the day. I find it by listening to spiritual music, by reading spiritual books, by going to the Adoration Chapel. I find it because I am continually seeking it and because I try to stay near to God with a soul that is pure and clear of sin...I have the Sacrament of Penance available to me whenever I stray and God speaks to me through this Sacrament. He brings me back to Himself, so that I once again live in His good grace. Yes, I am so weak of myself, but so strong when I am near to Him. He is my rich mine and I am at rest with Him through the Sacraments.

#3. "Though the path is plain and smooth for people of good will, those who walk it will not travel far, and will do so only with difficulty if they do not have good feet, courage, and tenacity of spirit."

I can long for God, for goodness, for heaven,…but the only way to gain God, or goodness, or heaven is through the virtue of fortitude, which will uphold our souls in time of trouble and adversity, and which will sustain our efforts after holiness. What does it mean to "have good feet"? I believe it means that we can never slow down in our effort to reach God, in our effort to acquire holiness, goodness, peace. Tenacity of spirit means to me that we must stick to our purpose, and never, ever give in to the temptations of the world, which surround us constantly.

Each day I renew my determination to do good, to acquire virtue, to love God more than ever before. But with each new day comes new trials, such as I've never before experienced. It isn't easy to live a virtuous life…to love God more than anything else. I'm often faced with new trials that I never experienced before, and I do not know how to face these trials. My pride wants to avoid them, since it is determined to become a saint, but these new trials just don't seem to fit into the pattern I have drawn up for myself.

I presume to be much holier than I really am, and my spirit shrinks away from so heavy a trial. I say to myself, "After all, I am trying to become holy. Doesn't he or she know that? How can they say this to me? How can they overlook my goodness to the point of affronting me so?" Yes, our spirit will tend to shrink away from some of these heavy trials, and we will feel that we have lost ground in our effort to become a saint.

And yet, we find hope in the realization that God knows us inside and out. He knows of our valiant effort towards holiness, even though the world does not know. With this knowledge, we can face almost any trial with courage, and yes, with tenacity of spirit. We will eventually, over time, become stronger because of having faced this particular trial. Even though our pride may have been deeply offended, we will come to see that it doesn't matter what other people think of us. The only thing that matters is that God sees our purity of intention, for God alone is the person we want to please. God sees our souls suffering, and if we dare to ask His help, we will find that He is always there for us, always defending us, always uplifting us to Himself. "If you do not fear falling alone, do you presume that you will rise up alone?"

#9. "Consider how much more can be accomplished by two than by one alone."

If you are a nun or a priest or brother, you will probably not have a problem finding a Spiritual Director. But, if you are a lay person, it is often very difficult to find one. Because it is so important, I suggest you pray very hard. God will hear your prayers, and if He sees fit, you will find one. Traveling on the Spiritual Path is often very difficult… it is a path strewn with obstacles. It is not impossible to walk the path alone, for God is always with you, but it is much safer to walk the path with a guide. You will feel so much safer if there is a spiritual person to guide you. Once you start seriously to tread this path, you will discover that there are many difficulties which come your way. Often there are decisions you must make. It is foolishness to think that you can make these decisions on your own, without anyone's help. The spiritual path is a long and winding road, and often we get lost when we try to go it alone.

I found my Spiritual Director in a very unusual way. In the fall of 2011 the Convent I was in during the year 1961 was holding a 50 year reunion for all of the women who had been in the Novitiate with me. When I went to the reunion, I discovered that one of my classmates was a Spiritual Director, and so I wrote to her and asked if she would be my Director. She suggested we do it over the phone. She calls me once a month and we talk for an hour. This has been a tremendous help to me, for she gives me good advice, is very interested in my spiritual journey, and sets goals for me. She gives me very much needed and good advice. She ends our conversation with beautiful readings she has come across, which inspire me greatly.

Before this, I had been privileged to have a Priest for a Spiritual Director for many years. When this came to an end, I was lost and alone on my spiritual journey. After many months and years of prayer, once again God was good enough to provide me with my present Spiritual Director. I can't begin to say how much I benefit from this gift of God. The spiritual path is sometimes strewn with thorns and stones, and as we try to make our way along this path, there is no better assurance than for us to place our hand in that of another holy person—our Spiritual Guide. Once again we go forth securely, with one hand joined to him or her, in my case to a very holy Nun.

#12. "God desires the smallest degree of purity of conscience in you more than all the works you can perform."

Purity of conscience is something we should aim at as our highest goal. So many things get in the way. Our pride is one thing which leads us astray. We need to pray and ask God to help us be pure in all of our thoughts. He will help us to see whether or not we are acting out of pride. He will reveal to us all of the many side roads we are about to take. Are we doing this because we might end up feeling better about ourselves, or are we doing it because we love God and see this as a way of growing closer to Him?...of falling deeper in love with Him? It is good to examine our motives closely before acting. If we are imbued with the love of God, it follows that our actions will draw us nearer to Him. In any case, do all with a pure heart solely out of love for Him. As St. John of the Cross says, it will then be a greater act than all the other acts we can perform.

#14. "God values in you the inclination to dryness and suffering for love of Him more than all the consolations, spiritual visions, and meditations you could possibly have."

This saying is a difficult one to put into practice. It is part of our nature to wish for the sweetness of consolation rather than dryness and suffering. When we consider how lowly we are of ourselves, how we are as nothing, miserable and alone, it is only natural that we would seek to be brought out of our misery. Here we are being told just the opposite...that we should be seeking dryness and suffering for love of Him. It is a hard saying. It is the truth, and the truth will bring us closer to God than we could have ever imagined.

I find in my life experience that whenever everything is going well, when I have no health problems, no money problems, no problems in my family, I tend to lose sight of what is really important in life, and I become a little carefree and more careless in my spiritual pursuits. It is when people in my life experience greater problems and seek my help through prayer, that I realize how dependent we are upon God for every good, for every blessing. When I am asked to turn to God in prayer for the benefit of others, I begin to see how fragile my life is, and how fragile is everyone's life and well-being. When I turn my focus on God as the source of all good, I become closer to Him with less tendency to rely on myself and my weaker nature.

We will eventually, over time, become stronger because of having faced this particular trial. Even though our pride may have been deeply offended, we will come to see that it doesn't matter what other people think of us. The only thing that matters is that God sees our purity of intention, for God alone is the person we want to please. God sees our souls suffering, and if we dare to ask His help, we will find that He is always there for us, always defending us, always uplifting us to Himself.

#15. "Deny your desires and you will find what your heart longs for. For how do you know if any desire of yours is according to God?"

Oh my Good Lord, yes, how do I know if my desires are according to Your will? I think about some of my desires—

that my car will keep on running, that my computer will keep on working, that my daughters will each have a good and productive life, that my doctors will keep me in good health, and on and on. When I stop to think about this, I realize I should have one desire only—that I do the will of God in all things…that I accept His will for me, no matter what that might be. If I open my heart to God, and let Him know that I am willing to suffer anything for the love of Him, then all of my desires disappear, and I wait upon the Lord to see what He wishes for me, and how He leads me in this life towards one goal—to someday be with Him in heaven. When I'm thinking and praying in this way, all of my worldly desires vanish, and I long for only one thing—to search for God in everything I do—to do His will in all things. And how do I know that will—His will? I try to know Gods' will by being attentive to the things He has surrounded me with—Holy Mass, spiritual music, spiritual reading. It is through these that I come to know His will. If I start to become worried or agitated about something, I immediately recognize that I have strayed from seeking His will alone. For Gods' ways are not our ways. God does not want us to worry or to be upset about little or big things. No, God wants for us to have a peaceful heart. Anything that destroys our inner peace is not from God, and it means we have strayed from seeking and doing His will. In my everyday activities, I can either be happy and peaceful, or I can let outside influences destroy my inner peace. When that happens, I turn my attention to God and humbly ask Him to see His will for me, so that I can regain my peace.

#18. "The soul that carries within itself the least appetite for worldly things bears more unseemliness and impurity in its journey to God than if it were troubled by all the hideous and annoying temptations and darknesses describable;…for, so long as it does not consent to these temptations, a soul thus tried can approach God confidently, by doing the will of His majesty, who proclaims: *Come to me, all you who labor and are heavily burdened, and I will refresh you. (Mt. 11:28)"*

Which one of us can actually say we do not have the least appetite for worldly things? I know I can say that I am not at all rich, but I am surrounded by things I consider the necessities of life. Am I willing to part with them if the Lord should ask this of me? For example, my bed, or my recliner, or my computer, or my books or CD's? All these little material things help me live a full and rich life. Am I willing to give them up for the love of God, if He should ask this of me? And yet I hear these words—"the soul that carries within itself the least appetite for worldly things…" I am so richly blessed with the necessities of life. There are millions of people around the world not so richly blessed. I often think of this fact, and am then overwhelmed at the abundance of wealth I am blessed with, even though I am considered to be below the poverty level. What do riches and wealth mean to me? Nothing. I consider wealth a hindrance along the pathway to God, for I believe it draws people to put their trust in things rather than in God.

I cannot say enough about poverty of spirit—a desire for nothing of this world, but only for the things of God. How I long for spiritual riches—for virtues, for the gift of prayer and contemplation, for the ability to love the least of God's brethren—the poor, the hungry, the starving, prisoners, veterans of wars, and on and on. All these people are precious in the eyes of God and should be precious to me as well. Sometimes I'm faced with a decision to give what is left over at the end of the month to the needy, or to my daughter, who is struggling. I then choose to give to my daughter, even though this means I give less to the needy. I ask for Your Wisdom, oh Lord. I make a decision to give to someone I know and love, instead of giving to someone who may be dying. Will You hold me accountable for this decision, or will You comfort me? I don't always know Your will, my Lord, and so I do what makes me feel at peace. I allow You to be my Judge, my most merciful Judge. I trust in Your mercy, knowing that You know what is deep in my heart. You know me inside and out, and because of this, I don't fear Your judgment.

#21. "The pure and whole work done for God in a pure heart merits a whole kingdom for its owner."

I must examine my heart on a daily basis, even on an hourly basis. Am I doing at this time exactly what God wants me to be doing? How do I know if I have a pure heart? I don't ever really know for certain, but if God is calling me to do His will and I do otherwise, I'm just not comfortable with myself. I feel God's grace calling from within to do what He wants me to do, even if it's something I would rather not do at this time. Then, when I submit to His will, my heart burns within me with His love, with His approval. Yes, the Lord can let us know in various ways just what He is calling us to do. We must learn to be attuned to His will at all times. By doing God's will at every moment, we do inherit a whole kingdom. Our hearts burn within us with love, peace, and joy. There is nothing in the world to compare with this.

#22. "A bird caught in birdlime has a twofold task: It must free itself and cleanse itself. And by satisfying their appetites, people suffer in a twofold way: They must detach themselves and, after being detached, clean themselves of what has clung to them."

Oh how true this is. I was attached to a person in my family who was going through a hard time. I lived her life vicariously, suffering probably far more than she suffered. My thoughts were constantly about her. I thought of nothing else, and prayed for her continuously. On looking back upon this situation, I see that I was unduly attached to her, and that I must free myself of this worry, or I would never become close to God. Little by little, I practiced detachment, and discovered how much had clung to me. It took me a long time to detach, but I began to notice that when I stopped worrying, nothing bad happened. This person was happy to be free of me, and I was happy to be free of her. My worry was useless, and when I realized this, I turned to prayer instead. Now I place her totally in the arms of the Loving God, whom I know loves her far more than I ever would or could love her. I will not say that it was easy for me to detach. It was probably the most difficult thing I'll ever have to do, but with God's help, all things are possible. I praise and thank the Lord for giving me the grace to finally detach.

As time goes on, I am once again tempted to be caught in this trap, this birdlime. It is then that I must make an effort to detach, over and over again if I must, in order to stay free to love God above every human being, even when that person is one of my children whom I love very dearly. In other words, this is not a one-time decision. It is a decision I must make over and over, on a daily basis. It is not easy to detach from someone we love so dearly, but detach we must, not only for our own benefit but also for the benefit of that individual. We must learn to allow others, especially those we love, to become autonomous and to learn to care for themselves. That is a great gift to give to someone we love, in fact, the greatest gift we can give to them.

#23. "Those who do not allow their appetites to carry them away will soar in their spirit as swiftly as the bird that lacks no feathers."

I realize that I must keep a constant watch over my appetites. When I make small or big sacrifices as my way of prayer and penance, I find that my appetites are so much less, and I feel so much freer. When I can say no to something I love, for a way of prayer, I soar in spirit, and am drawn more closely to the loving God, for He becomes the one and only thing I desire in this life. Anything that gives me earthly pleasure only seems to draw me away from this pure love of God. By not giving into my worldly desires or pleasures, I have more room for God in my life. I am drawn more surely to the safety of being nearer to God.

#24. "The fly that clings to honey hinders its flight, and the soul that allows itself attachment to spiritual sweetness hinders its own liberty and contemplation."

Ah yes! It is so easy and tempting to cling to spiritual sweetness. Which one of us does not relish the gifts of God? We must set ourselves free of this kind of attachment. When God chooses to lavish His sweetness upon us, we must be careful not to cling to it as though it is something we've earned. It is pure gift! We can feel free to accept this gift, but we must also be strong enough to let it go, and not to seek it again, so that we are open, not only to receiving favors from the Lord but also to receive the Cross. It is the cross that gives us growth and strength and proves our love for God. As in Psalm 43, we can say "Why are you cast down, my soul, why groan within me? Hope in God; I will praise Him still, my savior and my God."2

There are so many ways in which we can cling to honey. I am a very vain person and much of my clinging is to compliments of one kind or another. I find myself "setting up" myself to gain a compliment. When it comes, I bask in its' sweetness. When it doesn't come, I am disappointed. I'm learning to discern this fault in myself and to not let it happen. This may be a lifetime goal, a goal that I may never achieve fully in my lifetime. If I am aware of this fault and discover that on my own I can't get rid of it, I will try to remember to give it to God. With God's help we can grow and achieve our goals.

> #25. "Withdraw from creatures if you desire to preserve, clear and simple in your soul, the image of God. Empty your spirit and withdraw far from them and you will walk in divine lights, for God is not like creatures."

What a hard saying this is, and yet so true! How do I withdraw from my family, my friends? Even though it is very difficult, I believe I must do this if I am to become closer to God. I must still live my life among them—family and friends—but all of my waking thoughts should not center around them but instead, around God. I can only do this with God's help, and so I cry out in my soul, "Help me, O Lord. Give me strength and courage to do Your will in all things... help me to know Your will in all things." Psalm 42 says it best..."Like the deer that yearns for running streams, so my soul is yearning for You, my God. My soul is thirsting for God, the God of my life; when can I enter and see the face of God?"3

I have a long-time friend, with whom I shared everything that happened during my waking day. I have come to realize that this is not a good thing for me. By doing this, I forget to acknowledge God's part in my day and to thank God for all the graces He has bestowed upon me that day. By sharing with a friend...by opening my soul to him, I tend to forget that all these little treasures actually come from God, and I need to lock them within my heart and share them with no one but God Himself. If I really, truly want to be close to God, I will keep silence about many things, about the many gifts God has given to me. I will spend my day with the Lord, thanking Him for His goodness to me, sharing my sorrows with Him alone, and doing everything in my power to become one with Him. When I do this, I come to the realization that all good comes from Him, and that if I am sorely tested, that, too comes from God for my own growth and holiness. As St. John of the Cross says—"Empty your spirit and withdraw far from them and you will walk in divine lights, for God is not like creatures."4

#26. "Who can free themselves from lowly manners and limitations if You do not lift them Yourself, my God, in purity of love? How will human beings begotten and nurtured in lowliness rise up to You, Lord, if You do not raise them with Your hand that made them?"

Oh my God, how, indeed, will I free myself from the things of this world if You do not help me? How will I become holy if You Yourself do not help me to be holy? I am involved in all manners of activity, striving to do Your will and to become closer to You, but I fail so often. I get bogged down with thoughts of this material world. Right now I am obsessed with getting rid of debt, even though it be a minor debt. What I really need to do is to budget to the best of my ability, so that I can pay off the debt, and then to think nothing more about it. Oh my Lord, I am so weak, so miserable. I want to do nothing but Your will, and yet I am often tempted to reach out to others and help them financially. When will I learn that I can't do this without going further in debt? When will I learn to say "no"? For me, it is easier to give than to receive. That is because I love so much and hate to see other people hurting. But I do not have riches or wealth to be able to give freely. As difficult as it is, I must listen to my counselor, and think of myself first in many situations. You have provided me with a wonderful counselor and a wonderful spiritual director. Please give me the grace and wisdom to follow their advice. God did not give me the means to be a philanthropist. I must sit back and take into account what I have to give and what would be foolish for me to give.

Another way of looking at this problem is to see where I can cut back on my expenses. I'm learning that there are ways of cutting back, so as to leave me with a little extra—an ability to give to those less fortunate than myself. I am not happy unless I can share my good fortune with the less fortunate.

#26. "With what procrastinations do you wait, since from this very moment you can love God in your heart?"

Yes, from this very moment, I can love God in my heart. I can say "I love You," but I don't always know how to show my love for Him. I think of little things I can do for Him. People tend to give me food, because they know that I am poor. Many times, it is food not according to my taste, and I am tempted to throw it out. But as a person seeking to do penance for the love of God, I eat everything given to me, whether I like it or not. This is just one small example of how I show my love for God. I believe God asks penance of us, and so I seek ways of doing penances. Many people think I am strange, but that is because they don't understand the concept of penance—that it is another form of prayer. For me, penance is taking up my cross and carrying it in union with Jesus Christ carrying His cross on Calvary. When I pray for someone, I also do penance as part of my prayer, mainly because in this way I am uniting myself with Christ on the cross, to suffer along with Him. I do believe that penance greatly enhances our prayer. When I begin to pray, I think of all the sinners in the world, and what a sorry state they are in, and most of them don't even know it. I pray that sinners become aware of their sins, and respond to the call to repentance. If I could save only one sinner, I believe my life would be worthwhile. But I am not happy to stop there—I want to save many sinners, in whatever way I can, whatever way is possible for me. I have been given such grace, so as to understand the consequences of sin, and the benefits of grace. Oh that the world would understand this. My heart bleeds when I think of how many people are living sinful lives. And if my heart bleeds, then how much more does Our Savior's heart bleed, He Who gave His life on the Cross to save mankind? He did this because of His great love for each and every one of us. How often do we turn our back on this gracious Lover? How He must suffer to see so many sinners turn away from Him and refuse His grace.

If I suffer because a loved one turns his back on Christ, how much must Christ Himself suffer...He Who loves us so very much that He underwent so much torture and pain? And He would have suffered this for only one person, as that is the extent of His love for each one of us. How can I turn my back on such a lover? How can I not feel the greatest remorse for my action when such action is sinful? Oh Lord, let me never sin again!

#26. "You will not take from me, my God, what You once gave me in Your only Son, Jesus Christ, in Whom You gave me all I desire. Hence, I rejoice that if I wait for You, You will not delay."

Oh Lord, when You gave me Your Son You gave me everything I could possibly ask for. I treasure this gift beyond all gifts. I would give my life for this if it were taken away. Someday, perhaps we will be asked to give our life for this gift. If the time ever comes when we are asked to make the final sacrifice, please grant us the grace, the fortitude, to give our lives graciously, and heroically. Don't let me falter—for I know what waits for me in the beyond—an eternity of bliss—a place in heaven around Your mighty throne.

#28. "The very pure spirit does not bother about the regard of others or human respect, but communes inwardly with God, alone and in solitude as to all forms, and with delightful tranquility, for the knowledge of God is received in divine silence."

My Dear Lord, I am trying very hard to become this "pure spirit", but I am not there yet. I still talk to others about my spiritual life and even tell others about the sacrifices I am making. When I catch myself doing this, I hang my head in shame, for then I am seeking praise from mortal men rather than doing things solely for love of You. It is my goal, my dream, that someday I will be so engrossed in love of You that I won't care what others think of me. I will do everything hidden from the outside world, as though I were a hermit. I long for this day, Lord, when I will be so in love with You that it won't even enter my head to share my acts with another person. Instead, I will hide any good I do from others so that I will be doing everything for You alone. I love You, Lord, so much that I want to live my life solely for love of You and totally give of myself without seeking any reward or recognition. I believe this will happen only when I have become holy and only when You have granted me the graces of holiness. A loving, gentle, meek and patient soul is always easy to get along with. Nothing can be said that will hurt their pride and so we don't need to be fearful when associating with them. That soul will make us feel like we are the only person in the world they are concerned about and we can be sure of their love.

#29. "A soul enkindled with love is a gentle, meek, humble, and patient soul."

Love will be the embodiment of these virtues. If I love everyone who comes into my life I will be gentle, so that I will treat that person with the greatest kindness and respect. I will not try to rise above that person in pride, but practice meekness so as to make him or her feel wholly trusting of me. Be it a child or an adult, I will try to be as gentle as though he or she were a baby. I know this isn't always easy but if I beg the Lord to clothe me with humility I will be able to practice patience no matter what happens. Through love, I can practice patience with anyone I have contact with, always seeing beyond the outer person and looking deep into their soul.

#33. "I didn't know you, my Lord, because I still desired to know and relish things."

Oh how true this is. As long as I desire "things", my attention strays from You to things of the world. I cannot love both—I cannot have both. I strive very hard not to desire anything that I don't have, even if it is of great importance. For example, I have a car and it takes a lot of my attention to keep it running. I've come to the conclusion that when my car starts to "die", I will let go of it, and will plan my life, not around it but rather on how I can get along without it. This will be a life-changing event for me, but I am ready to go without it if it starts taking up too much of my attention or money. Other things which I no longer pay any attention to are clothes and food. I try very hard to get along without buying new clothes, and when it comes to food I try to sacrifice so that I am not always thinking about what to have for my next meal. I've learned how to get along with less, even though I may have to go to bed hungry. I often reflect on how fortunate I am to have enough food to eat when I know so many people in the world do not have enough food or water. When I reflect in this way, I no longer think of food as that important. I try to get along with less rather than with more.

#34. "Well and good if all things change, Lord God, provided we are rooted in you."

Oh my Lord, right now everything in my life is good. I am an American, and as a citizen of a free country I am free to worship You as I please. If this should ever change and my freedom was taken away, let me be so rooted in You that I would give my life for You. My physical and spiritual needs are taken care of, because I am on SS and SSI. If this were to change, and I would have no source of income, my life would be in shambles. Oh Lord, if I were to have no place to live, no doctors to take care of my needs, no medicine, etc. let me always depend totally on You to care for me. And if I am called to suffer in this manner, let me think of all the saints and how much they suffered for You. Let me be willing to suffer anything and everything for the love of You. Right now I have everything I need of a material nature. Perhaps this will not always be so. I picture myself without the medical help I now have and can't help but wonder how I would survive without it. And yet, so many of Your saints had no such help, and so many of them died at a young age. I am already past the age of most of Your saints. Therefore, I cannot claim that I have any rights. My only wish is to accept whatever comes my way with joy and submission to Your holy will. I am willing to suffer for Your sake, Lord, anything that You ask of me. All

I ask is that You give me the strength I need to suffer and die for You!

#38. "Reflect that your guardian angel does not always move you to desire for an action, but he does always enlighten your reason. Hence, in order to practice virtue do not wait until you feel like it, for your reason and intellect are sufficient."

Oh Lord, there are many times when I do not feel like practicing virtue. At these dry times, when my good will seems to be dried up, give me the grace to overcome my feelings and to do Your will in all things, at all times. Teach me to follow my reason and intellect, which lead me to do what You wish for me to do. Today is one of those days. I have made a commitment to visit a lonely man, and to try and make his monotonous life less boring and more interesting. I usually visit him with much enthusiasm and goodwill, but today, for some reason, I don't feel so inclined. And so, I turn to You, my Lord, to lead me and to guide me so that I may be cheerful inside and out, and that I hide all feelings of distaste of discomfort. I can only do this with Your grace and Your strength, Your love and good will. If I am open to Your will in all things, I will see many opportunities for practicing virtue. Not only will I see them but I will be motivated to act on them. I never know how long I will be capable, since I am getting pretty old, so I must seize every chance I get for doing good for others. I envision a life where I help others in every way that is possible for me, whether I feel like it or not.

#40. "What you most seek and desire you will not find by this way of yours, nor through high contemplation, but in much humility and submission of heart."

I am learning to accept where the Lord has placed me, not in high contemplation but still enjoying mental prayer. I pray daily that someday God will give me the gift of contemplation, but I recognize that I still don't have that gift, and so, rather than be remorseful about this fact, I'm learning to be where the Lord wants me to be...at His feet, learning His ways slowly and gradually, asking always for humility and submission. I find great joy in this place at His feet, knowing that someday He will call me to higher forms of prayer. At this time in my life I submit totally to His wish for me. I feel that He is drawing me very slowly into this prayer for which I long, but realize it is only when He wills it for me that I will realize it. It is totally up to God and I accept that fact. I will never stop praying for this gift, but at the same time I will make use of the present gift and will offer up to God my entire will. When He deems it fitting to draw me more closely to Him I will submit my entire being into His loving care.

#41. "Do not tire yourself, for you will not enter into the savor and sweetness of spirit if you do not apply yourself to the mortification of all this that you desire."

Yes, Lord, I will apply myself to the mortification of my desires in every way possible. It is only when I succeed in doing this that I feel at one with You, for I realize that You want us to practice mortification to the greatest extent possible. I try to mortify my appetite for things which other people take for granted, such as not to watch much TV, not to eat certain foods for which I have a great appetite, and to greatly limit spending money for things I don't really need. When I practice this, I find much greater joy in the simple things life has to offer. Everything seems as gift to me and I find great joy in all the little things life has to offer.

I have to admit that I am rich in the fact I have everything I need to lead a happy and wholesome life. I must keep reminding myself of the fact that the majority of people in the world are not so blessed, and I should look for opportunities to help them. Opportunities abound—and it is for me to take these opportunities to give what I can to help others, not expecting a thank you in return. My thanks come in the fact I live with great peace of mind and heart, knowing that I have given until it hurts.

> #42. "Reflect that the most delicate flower loses its' fragrance and withers fastest; therefore guard yourself against seeking to walk in a spirit of delight, for you will not be constant. Choose rather for yourself a robust spirit, detached from everything, and you will discover abundant peace and sweetness, for delicious and durable fruit is gathered in a cold climate."

Oh my most gracious Lord, how true this is. I so long to be detached from everything—from all the goods of the earth, from worry about those I love, from desire for contentment, from thoughts about my health and well-being. I find that when I am free from worry about any of these things my joy is the greatest. I honestly don't desire anything but that which is Your will for me. I recognize that Your will is not always what I will. No, sometimes reality is harsh and the world is distasteful. It is at these times that I am brought to seek You, oh gracious and hidden Lord. Our ways are not Your ways and it is only when we see this and submit ourselves to Your ways that we find great happiness and great peace.

#44. "Be attentive to your reason in order to do what it tells you concerning the way to God. It will be more valuable before your God than all the works you perform without this attentiveness and all the spiritual delights you seek."

A short time ago I thought the Lord was asking something of me which seemed impossible. I finally came to the point of listening to my reason, and only then did I realize that God never asks the impossible of us. I decided to do my best to please God, and after that, to realize what I couldn't do. God placed within my heart a flaming desire to pray for purity and chastity in the world. My first thought was that I was somehow supposed to change the whole world. After considering it for some time, I decided to write a letter and send it and an e-mail to everyone I know. After I had done that, I decided that I could do no more, but that I should pray very hard for these virtues to grow in the hearts of men and women around the world. I have a great faith in the power of prayer, and so I will continue to pray that these virtues are placed on the hearts of men and women throughout the world.

#45. "Blessed are they who, setting aside their own pleasure and inclination, consider things according to reason and justice before doing them."

I believe that every minute of the day I should try to do God's will rather than my own. Being that I am an older person, I am rather limited as to what I can do. And yet, upon listening to the Lord, I am led to doing things I never thought possible. Because of this, my life touches the lives of many people. I believe God asks me to do things through the lips of others, His servants, and because of that, I hardly ever say no. My friends, who are close to my age, envy me for the variety I have in my life. I believe God wants me to live a very active life, and yet leads me in my quiet hours to strive for a life of contemplation. I answer His beck and call to do the ordinary things in life and to seek for the extra-ordinary life of prayer where I believe God is leading me.

> #49. "If you purify your soul of attachments and desires, you will understand things spiritually. If you deny your appetite for them, you will enjoy their truth, understanding what is certain in them."

How do I purify myself of attachments and desires? For one thing, I've decided that I must live on a strict budget so that I can help other suffering people in the world. When I eat, I make sure to eat all the food that is given to me, whether I like it or not. This helps me to save money on groceries. Eventually, I will find myself ahead financially, and will be able to help the poor, the starving, and the veterans. I feel called to help in a very restricted measure, for I do not have much to give. And yet, I believe in giving until it hurts. Whenever I fix my meals, I keep in mind how many people in the world would die for such food, and I relish it all the more while giving thanks to God that I have not had to suffer hunger and thirst like so many people in this world. In this way, I purify my desires. I don't spend time wishing for new clothes, or more shoes, or rich jewelry, etc. No, I am far beyond that, to the point where I no longer read the ads, so that I will not enkindle within myself desires for things I don't need. Because of this, I lead a very simple life, getting along basically without any excess. It is true that because of this I am led to a greater understanding of what life is really about. I am set free from longings and yearnings for things. My days are filled, rather, with thoughts of God and of heaven for which I long.

#51. "That person has truly mastered all things who is not moved to joy by the satisfaction they afford or saddened by their insipidness."

I believe that we should not over-react when something good has happened to us, nor should we be sad if things don't turn out our way and we are greatly disappointed. Instead, we should temper our happiness and in our sadness we should turn to God for assistance and comfort rather than allowing ourselves to become sad or depressed.

I applied this saying to the outcome of a court case, where the person in question was very close to me, and I didn't want to see her get jail time. I had to control my feelings to a very great degree, so that I wouldn't even allow the person in question know how deeply I felt. I controlled my fears by not saying anything to her about my fears. It all turned out well in the end, but I had geared myself to accepting anything, even the most distasteful outcome. By acting in this way I actually saved myself a lot of grief.

#52. "If you wish to attain holy recollection, you will do so not by receiving but by denying."

Oh my Lord, I wish to be so recollected that I see You in every event of my day and I grasp onto Your strength to help me get through the day. Naturally there are moments of darkness when I cannot see the light or the good in the events of the day. During these moments I cling to You as to a boat sinking in the roughest sea. I place all my trust in You to help me get through the really rough times. This only happens when I deny my will and come to accept Your will, even sometimes when all I see is darkness.

I also think that one can attain holy recollection by looking about to see nature in all its array. Even sitting here at my desk next to the window I look out and see the ever-changing sky, the intricate leaves and branches on the trees, the people who pass by—usually little children because I am right next to a school. I look and reflect and pray with gratitude for a God Who created all of this and so much more. Will I ever be able to amply give thanks for these blessings and so many more that I can't begin to count them?

#54. "Souls will be unable to reach perfection who do not strive to be content with having nothing, in such fashion that their natural and spiritual desire is satisfied with emptiness; for this is necessary in order to reach the highest tranquility and peace of spirit. Hence, the love of God in the pure and simple soul is almost continually in act."

How shall I be content to have nothing, my Lord? All that I possess seems so important to me. And yet, I become aware of the multitudes of refugees who have to leave everything they own behind them to try and reach a safer country. Along the way, they are placed in tents and wait in these tents for years, looking forward to someday being called forth for a new chance at life. How many of them never receive this summons and in the time of waiting, many of them die from a lack of nutrition and from disease. What do they own? Nothing. They sleep on the floor, or rather on the dirt floor. They do not have the things we take for granted...chairs, stove, cupboards, utensils, pots and pans, or even water. No, they only have the clothes on their back, and yet they rejoice that they have escaped their attackers. It is hard to imagine the kind of life they lead, just waiting for an invitation to a better form of life. How do I merit to have all my needs met and hope for the future? I do not take my life for granted. I so appreciate the fact that my doctor looks out for all of my physical needs by ordering many different tests. At 72 years old, I feel so much younger because of all the good medical care I receive. Did I earn it in any way? No. I just happened to be born in an affluent society, where the elderly are treated with great care and respect. As for my spiritual desires, I try to be satisfied with emptiness so that I can reach the highest tranquility and peace of spirit. Because of this, the love of God within me is almost continually in act. It is hard to believe, but the more I place myself in God's presence, the love of God is there waiting for me continually. How greatly blessed I am, through no merit of my own.

#56. "The soul that journeys to God, but does not shake off its' cares and quiet its' appetites, is like one who drags a cart uphill."

My Dearest Lord, on my journey to You I must learn to cast off my cares and quiet my appetites. When I lose myself in worry and stress, I am in a state of disquiet and tend to be constantly upset. It is only when I put aside my desires and am totally accepting of my place in life that I am at peace. I will add, this is not an easy task. I become so engrossed in making a living and in trying to succeed in life that I have no time or effort left over for the things of God. Please help me, Dear Lord, to stop all worry about extraneous things and to concentrate totally on You. If I could put this into practice, I could live like an angel, never mindful of the things of this earth but constantly living according to the maxims of St. John of the Cross.

#58. "This way of life contains very little business and bustling, and demands mortification of the will more than knowledge. The less one takes of things and pleasures the farther one advances along this way."

My Lord, I find myself today worrying about my livelihood. I must mortify my will, and make a firm decision not to worry but to put everything into Your hands. Each worried thought takes the place of an act of love for You and trust in You. Yes, it takes a lot of strength to mortify my will and yet I must if I wish to be free of attachment to worldly things. If things don't turn out to my advantage and I don't have the means to support myself, I will be willing to accept whatever You have in mind for me, my Lord, even if it means I am to be homeless.

What is most important to me is that I am following Your will at every moment. And how do I know Your will for me? It becomes more and more evident to me as I grow in prayer and stay close to You in daily Mass and Communion. How grateful I am that You provide for me the ability to attend daily Mass and how greatly this has changed my whole outlook on life. Mortification of the will is not easy...much harder than mortification of the senses. To mortify the senses, all I have to do is to say no. To mortify my will, I must first be able to discern what it is that I am striving after, and this is not always easy. I have run halfway down the trail before I am even aware of where I am going. Discerning my will is not always easy, but I must first recognize it before I can put a stop to it. By giving up my will I find myself growing closer to God...advancing along His way, which is all I care about.

> #59. "Think not that pleasing God lies so much in doing a great deal as in doing it with good will, without possessiveness and human respect."

No, I don't have to do a great deal to win God over. What little I do I must do with good will, wishing to please God, and not worrying about what other people will think of me. Also, what I do for God must not be done with possessiveness. I learned that today, as today was my first day of giving out Communion at the hospital. To me, this seemed like a great ministry, only to be told that this day was already covered by someone else, and the person asking me to do it made a mistake and wondered whether I would be willing to do home visits instead. My answer was that I was willing to go wherever God wanted me. This wouldn't earn me such a great reward interiorly, but since

I'm doing it totally because I see it as God's will for me, I am willing to change my course according to God's will and to do it most willingly.

The same holds for other things I do, such as my art work or my leadership role in "Faith in Recovery". I know I am not a good artist, but I so enjoy working with other people and in so doing, sometimes I end up creating something others like. I don't take the credit because I know it is a gift from God, be it ever so small a gift. As for leadership ability, I believe I am completely lacking in it. I continue to help out with the group because the people who come are needy and in want of help. I can see God working through us, the leaders, in spite of ourselves. I believe this is God's work and that we are merely the instruments through which God chooses to help those with pressing problems.

> #60. "When evening comes, you will be examined in love. Learn to love as God desires to be loved and abandon your own ways of acting."

I try to discern the ways God would have me act and I find it is not easy. So often I have to abandon my ways and find a better way of doing things—God's way, which is not always as easy as my way would have been. Not only is God's way sometimes more difficult—it also demands more from me—more effort, more humility, more acceptance and more resilience.

I realize that "when evening comes" refers to when I am dying. At that time I will be examined in love. Sometimes I feel as though I love too much. That is because I worry about those whom I love. I am going to try not to worry, but instead, to place all of my loved ones in God's hands, knowing that every one of them is so loved by God, so taken care of by Him, loved more than I could ever begin to fathom. Because I trust so much in the love of the Lord I have no reason to ever fear or be solicitous about my loved ones. Instead, I can place them very securely in His hands and get rid of every inclination to worry. By so doing, my life goes so much more smoothly and I am so much happier.

> #62. "Because the virtues you have in mind do not shine in your neighbor, do not think that your neighbor will not be precious in God's sight for reasons that you have not in mind."

It is very important to keep this truth in the forefront of my mind. Because of my frail human nature I look at others through a tainted lens. What I need to do is to stay away from judging anyone—my family, my friends, my acquaintances, and to try and see them through God's eyes, if that were possible. I have a tendency to judge others and I fear that God is not pleased when I do this. Yes, I've caught myself doing this several times. When I become aware of it I catch myself and realize how totally wrong I am and have been in the past. Now that the Lord has made me aware of this fault, I find that I'm much better able to love those whom I once judged unfairly. God wants me to be a generous lover, and to be kind in all of my judgments.

#64. "See that you are not suddenly saddened by the adversities of this world, for you do not know the good they bring, being ordained in the judgments of God for the everlasting joy of the elect."

Oh how much I tend to be saddened by the adversities of this world. I need to remember this,...that I do not know the good they will bring in the future. Upon looking back at my life, I reflect that I have suffered much due to the mental illness I suffered with for many years. Now that I am older and all of that is behind me, I reflect upon the fact that it is through this suffering that I have come to the state I'm now in—a state of peace and joy, mainly because along the way I found God. I found Him through the help of professionals, and through a great effort on my part to learn and to cooperate and to do all the necessary things which pulled me through all of those hard times. I can attest to the fact that through all of this I have arrived at a state of joy indescribable! God has been with me through it all even though there were many dark years when I didn't, couldn't see Him.

Right now I am suffering from the adversity of this world with regard to my support. In order to avoid a scam, I had to change my account number. Because of this, I didn't receive my social security payment for the month. Rather than spend time worrying about this situation, I give it totally to the Lord. Even if I do not receive the money owed to me, I will not fret and worry. I will strive to manage my money the best I can, and will not be upset if things don't work out as they should. This will not be easy but I can get through it with God's help. It is only a small example of how I'm learning to put things into God's hands and to eliminate all worry.

#65. "Do not rejoice in temporal prosperity, since you do not know if it gives you assurance of eternal life."

I believe almost everyone in my country enjoys temporal prosperity. In contrast to us, there are many, many countries where the people do not have enough food to eat or water to drink, or a place to rest their head. I do believe that it is up to us to help these people in any way we can. If we ignore those who have nothing and if we don't help them in any way we can, God will hold us accountable at the end of our life. If we have been blessed in such a way that all our needs are met, woe to us if we don't look beyond ourselves and recognize those less fortunate. No, temporal prosperity does not give us assurance of eternal life. We must be generous with our prosperity, even to the point where it hurts, or we will be judged in the end, and we will find that we have failed seriously.

#66. "In tribulation, immediately draw near to God with trust, and you will receive strength, enlightenment, and instruction."

It is important to remember, in times of tribulation, that we need to draw near to God Who will help us in ways we are not always fond of. Perhaps God will not give us what we ask for, but He will always provide us with what we need in order to draw closer to Him. If we are open to God's will in our lives, we will receive strength and courage to go on, even in the face of heartbreak. We must seek help from God and He will give us enlightenment as to how we should act and instruction about what we need to do. God's ways are not always our ways, and so we must be open to His wisdom. In this way, we can be sure to draw ever closer to Him, and that is really all that matters.

> #67. "In joys and pleasures, immediately draw near to God in fear and truth, and you will be neither deceived nor involved in vanity."

It is during times of joy and pleasure that we are tempted to forget all about God. That is why we must make a special effort during these times to remember God and to thank Him for all the good that we experience. It is easy during these times to become vain, and to think we are better than we really are. This would be a tragedy—to lose sight of the fact that all good comes from God, and that of ourselves we are nothing and can do nothing good without God's continual help. In times of good fortune, we should be so grateful to God and think to share our good fortune with those who have little or nothing. If our fortune is of a spiritual nature, we must be on watch so that we do not presume to think we are better than we really are, but in all humility be watchful and careful to attribute all of our grace to God, its' source.

> #68. "Take God for your bridegroom and friend, and walk with him continually; and you will not sin and will learn to love, and the things you must do will work out prosperously for you."

Yes, God is my bridegroom and my friend. All of my good is from Him. I try to live with the constant awareness that He is always there for me, in times of good as well as in times of trouble. As my bridegroom, He is ever watchful and protects me from all harm. As my friend, I can entrust Him with all my secrets knowing He will safeguard them and treasure them. Like a friend, I know He is always there to help me in my need, and I need never doubt His love and concern for me. When I walk with Him always at my side, I will never be tempted to sin and will grow deeper and deeper in love with Him. I will be drawn into prosperity and to me this means that my life will always be in His hands, so I never have anything to fear.

> #70. "Abide in peace, banish cares, take no account of all that happens, and you will serve God according to His good pleasure, and rest in Him."

To me, this is one of the greatest thoughts—to abide in peace, banish cares, and take no account of all that happens. Whenever I find myself worrying about something, little or big, I catch myself and think of this. I immediately give my care to God, knowing and trusting that God will take care of everything and that I need not worry about it a bit. By doing this, I am serving God in a great way—I am trusting in Him totally. By trusting in Him implicitly, I will be serving Him according to His pleasure, and will be at rest in Him. I have experienced this time and time again. I am prone to worry a lot. By practicing this saying, I learn to let go of all of my worries, be they big or little, and I become a much more peaceful person. Yes, I rest in Him. I feel totally protected by God, the One I love so intensely.

I will say that when something tragic happens in my life, or in the lives of those I love, my first reaction is to panic and to say "oh no!" how can this be happening?" My thoughts continue along these lines and I tend to become depressed and filled with worry. My thoughts travel quickly to anticipate future gloom and I am tempted to despair. When I find myself succumbing to this hopeless state, I almost immediately spot what is occurring in my mind and I quickly respond with thoughts of hope and trust in God. This makes the impending doom disappear quickly. I see God's hand in this event and am led to trust in Him completely. Once I start to trust, all of my fears disappear and I feel the loving hands of God upon me. Needless to say, my fears are quelled and all the disquiet I am experiencing disappears amid a flood of hopeful and meaningful thoughts. I believe that through this experience and similar experiences, I am drawn to a deeper trust in God's loving ways and I bask under His gentle care and love for me.

#71. "Consider that God reigns only in the peaceful and disinterested soul."

It is this thought that puts me totally at rest—and I live totally in peace. If I want to live in God and have God in me, then I must live wholly in peace...I cannot allow myself to worry, about the big things or the little things. I must engage my mind in thoughts of God at all times, or whenever possible. With this constant presence of God, I find myself enjoying a peace indescribable no matter what is happening outside of me or around me. I believe the whole world could collapse and I would be unaware of it, so totally would I be imbued with the presence of God.

I believe that this peace and disinterest are gifts from God and can be acquired through developing a habit of the presence of God. All through my day I try to maintain this presence of God as taught by Brother Lawrence, who says

that "when God finds a soul awash with a living faith He pours
into it the fullness of His graces. There they flow like a torrent,
spreading themselves wherever there is an opening." #5

#72. "Although you perform many works, if you do not
deny your will and submit yourself, losing all solicitude
about yourself and your affairs, you will not make
progress."

Dear Lord, this is my favorite saying. I do perform works,
but I know You are asking more of me. You want me to deny
my will and submit myself to Your will. You want me to lose all
solicitude about myself and those I love. You want me to stop
worrying about my affairs, financial or otherwise. You want
me to stop worrying about the people I love, and to submit
myself totally, giving You of myself in total acceptance of
everything that happens in my life. This is a hard saying. But
if I love You, I will follow this Your will for me and for my
loved ones. I will never stop praying, but my prayers, urgent
though they be, will focus more on You and Your will than
on me and my will. Until I learn to do this, I will not make
progress in the spiritual life.

#73. "What does it profit you to give God one thing if
He asks of you another? Consider what it is God wants,
and then do it. You will as a result satisfy your heart
better than with something toward which you yourself
are inclined."

I must ponder carefully in trying to learn God's will for
me, because it often isn't what I am inclined to do. In trying
to discern God's will for me, I need to pray very hard and

to listen to what God speaks in my heart. In order to listen carefully, I need quiet time spent in a peaceful atmosphere. If I am troubled about something else, I must first settle that before coming to the Lord in prayer and quiet, seeking to know His will for me.

When we pray, let us pray to know Gods' will for us, and to have the courage and stamina to go forward by doing that which God leads us to do. Sometimes it is difficult to know exactly what God wants us to do and sometimes when we do know, His will is not the easier path to follow. So, we should pray not only to know His will but also to follow His will as carefully and precisely as is possible to us. In the words of St. Teresa of Avila, "…many remain at the foot of the mount who could ascend to the top…I repeat and ask that you always have courageous thoughts. As a result of them the Lord will give you grace for courageous deeds." #6

#76. "Do not rejoice vainly, for you know how many sins you have committed and you do not know how you stand before God; but have fear together with confidence."

I believe it is a bit difficult to have both fear and confidence at one and the same time. It is true that I do not know how I stand before God, but I am confident that I did my best to make good confessions, and I have great trust in that sacrament. When I consider the great mercy of God I gain confidence in such a loving, merciful God and my soul is put at peace. Trust outweighs fear.

#77. "Since, when the hour of reckoning comes, you will be sorry for not having used this time in the service of God, why do you not arrange and use it now as you would wish to have done were you dying?"

Oh my God, how I see so clearly that this life is but a moment when compared to eternity. How important it is that we live this "moment" well, to the very best of our ability. And yet it is true that of ourselves we can do nothing, but with the grace of God we can do all things. I try to live each moment as though it were my last. I try to serve God with all my heart and with all my strength. Yet, I know that of myself I can do nothing. And so I cry out to God continually, "Lord, please help me. Please give me the courage and ability to serve You well, to do all I can for You in this life so that I can live with You for all eternity. I long to share every moment of my life with others in the hope that I can lead them to You, oh Lord, the love of my life. Oh Lord, I long not only to be close to You, but to bring all people to You, to know, love and serve You, so that when they die, they will not be afraid but will rejoice that they have lived a good and wholesome life...a holy life in service of You."

#78. If you desire that devotion be born in your spirit and that the love of God and the desire for divine things increase, cleanse your soul of every desire, attachment, and ambition in such a way that you have no concern about anything. Just as a sick person is immediately aware of good health once the bad humor has been thrown off and a desire to eat is felt, so will you recover your health in God, if you cure yourself as was said.

Without doing this, you will not advance no matter how much you do."

My Lord, I do desire that my love for God and the desire for divine things increase. Because of my deep desire, I try to maintain a clean soul by keeping it free from every desire, attachment and ambition. I try to have no concern about **anything except about You, my Lord, and all things of a** spiritual nature. In the words of Elizabeth of the Trinity…"He placed within my heart a thirst for the Infinite and such a great need to love that He alone can satisfy it!" #7

> #79. "If you desire to discover peace and consolation for your soul and to serve God truly, do not find your satisfaction in what you have left behind, because in that which now concerns you you may be as impeded as you were before, or even more. But leave as well all these other things and attend to one thing alone that brings all these with it (namely, holy solitude, together with prayer and spiritual and divine reading), and persevere there in forgetfulness of all things. For if these things are not incumbent on you, you will be more pleasing to God in knowing how to guard and perfect yourself than by gaining all other things together; *what profit would there be for one to gain the whole world and suffer the loss of one's soul?* [Mt. 16:26]"

Lord, I do desire to discover peace and consolation for my soul, and to serve God truly. Because of my deep desire, I do not find satisfaction in worldly things, in things I have left behind. I must leave all these things and attend to one thing alone that brings all these with it (namely, holy solitude, together with prayer and spiritual and divine reading) and persevere there, forgetting all things. If I do this, I will be pleasing to God, and will know how to guard and perfect myself."

#80. "Bridle your tongue and your thoughts very much, direct your affection habitually toward God, and your spirit will be divinely enkindled."

Dear Lord, You ask us not only to be watchful of our tongue but also of our thoughts. If I listen to You carefully, I will see that You want our love continually. This gives me no room for my thoughts to stray far from You. You want me to think of You continually. This means that during all times of the day and night I should be thinking of You in whatever circumstances I find myself. As I grow closer to You, I realize that You want me all to Yourself. You don't want me to get caught up in the trivialities of everyday life and to worry about things needlessly. Instead, You want me to see You behind every activity of my day and night. I must be ever watchful in order to direct everything I do or say towards Your greater glory. I am learning to do this little by little, bit by bit. And when I succeed, my life becomes glorious. I am immersed in Your love and Your will and life goes so smoothly it is hard to even imagine. Thank You dearest Lord.

#81. "Feed not your spirit on anything but God. Cast off concern about things, and bear peace and recollection in your heart."

It is almost miraculous—how peaceful and recollected I can become when I do not think about anything, do not become concerned about anything but God. To arrive at this total peace and recollection, it may take many years of struggle and many futile attempts. But I am resolved to never give up trying. I believe that eventually this will become a way of life for me, and it could for anyone who tries. It sometimes seems impossible to have no concern about anything but God, but this is what Our Lord asks of us, and His promise is to set us free from all the worries of the world...free to think of Him constantly... to praise Him, to worship Him, to love Him alone.

> #82. "Keep spiritually tranquil in a loving attentiveness to God, and when it is necessary to speak, let it be with the same calm and peace."

It is definitely not easy to keep spiritually tranquil in a loving attentiveness to God, but if we do succeed, sometimes after years of trying, we will attain that calm and peace we so intimately desire. This will only happen if we watch our speech carefully and speak only with great calm and peace, mindful in everything we say that we are trying to speak with great love and care, depending on God's grace to fill us and to mend all of our empty spaces.

When we speak, let us try to maintain always great calm and peace. We can only do that if we are filled with the presence and grace of God, and only if we try always to speak with great care truth as we see it. Therefore we must make a great effort to know the truth about all things, especially about things which matter in our lives and in the lives of those we love.

#83. Preserve a habitual remembrance of eternal life, recalling that those who hold themselves the lowest and poorest and least of all will enjoy the highest dominion and glory in God."

I probably say the Apostle's Creed twenty or more times a day, because I recite the Divine Mercy Chaplet over and over, for about an hour each day. Whenever reciting the prayer, the Apostle's Creed, at the end of the Creed the words are "I believe in the forgiveness of sins, the resurrection of the body, and life everlasting. Amen." When I recite these words, I become immersed in awe and wonder to think that God is such a gracious and merciful God that He forgives all our sins, and raises our bodies from the dead to new life, to live happily with Him for all eternity. I can't help but wonder over what little I have done to earn such a fantastic reward! I ponder on the words "life everlasting" and am entirely mesmerized by the awesomeness of such a promise, and humility to recognize that God is such a merciful and loving God to reward us with this tremendous gift!

Those who hold themselves the lowest and purest and least of all will enjoy the highest dominion and glory in God. Yes, humility, humility, and again humility. Of course, we are the least and poorest of all, and as long as we see ourselves thus, we will benefit rewards for eternal life which are unbelievable—only the Angels and Saints know of this eternal realm, and we will someday reach these same heights if we can only remain immersed in humility, knowing ourselves to be the most undeserving of all.

#84. "Rejoice habitually in God, who is your salvation [Luke 1:47], and reflect that it is good to suffer in any way for him who is good."

Rejoice habitually in God, Who is "our" salvation. God is for us, and all around us. Because of this, depending upon our deep faith in Him, we can rejoice always, and at all times, in all things, no matter what happens to us or around us. Our faith in God is the key, and to hold this key we must continually place ourselves in God's loving care, believing in Him with all our heart and with all our might. I don't see how anyone who believes in God in this manner can ever be unhappy, for it is with this faith that we anticipate an eternity of bliss, living in the presence of this Almighty Father. We are to reflect on the fact that it is good to suffer in any way for Him Who is good. There are so many ways in which we suffer, but I think one of the worst or hardest sufferings would be to lose sight of the fact that God is always with us—ever near to us, in times of greatest hardships, and especially at times we lose our presence of God. It is precisely at this time that we should remind ourselves that He loves us at all times, in all circumstances, and we should turn our minds wholly on Him and see Him in every second, every moment, every hour of what sometimes might prove to be a long and uneventful day.

#85. "Have an intimate desire that His Majesty grant you what he knows you lack for his honor."

We should always ask God to fill our emptiness, to give us the virtues He knows we lack. We ask this of Him, not for our glory but for our benefit, so that we can become more like

Him, and so that we can grow closer to Him as our Lover. The virtues we lack are keeping us apart from Him. So often, we don't know what virtues we lack and so we pray that God will let us know so we can strive to grow in that particular virtue, and thus become closer and closer to God.

> #87. "Crucified inwardly and outwardly with Christ, you will live in this life with fullness and satisfaction of soul, and possess your soul in patience."

Oh my Lord, let me share in Your sufferings so that I can live this life with fullness and satisfaction of soul. Who am I to ask for a share in Your sufferings? How can I begin to bear them? It is because I know You will give me the strength I need that I ask for a share in Your sufferings. The world knows very little about such things. The world would frown upon me for asking such a thing. The world would think me "mad"! You let me know this great secret—that those who suffer the most are the closest to Your heart.

If I could, I would share this secret with all those I love, so they wouldn't fear the things this life brings in the way of trials and sufferings. I must admit that not many people think along these lines. Most people would do anything to avoid suffering. While that is a good and honorable thing, sufferings still manage to come our way no matter how hard we have tried to avoid them. I believe it is possible to be happy even in the midst of sufferings. The secret is to realize what we can gain eternity as our reward if we accept the cross and lift it up to the Lord, suffering in union with His sufferings and His horrible death. While suffering, we would try to join ours with His, with deep love and great submission. We can only do this with the help of His grace. And so, we must pray daily for the grace of accepting whatever cross Christ chooses for us…accepting it with love and humility, knowing its' power to draw us closer to Our Beloved.

> #88. "Preserve a loving attentiveness to God with no desire to feel or understand any particular thing concerning Him."

Oh, my Lord, I do not understand You. And yet, I do love You with all my heart. I do desire to feel and understand You, but realize that this will only take place when my entire heart and mind have been turned over to You—to Your loving care. I have no idea as to when or how this will happen but I hold myself in readiness for whatever You wish to share with me.

> #90. "Enter within yourself and work in the presence of Your Bridegroom, who is ever present loving you."

What a beautiful statement—your Bridegroom is ever present loving you. How can we become worried or dismayed over all the trivial things that make up our life? How can we worry about money matters, or friendships, or our children and grand-children? If we trust that God is our Bridegroom and ever loving us, would we not be completely at peace about the things of this world? Would we not be totally free of cares and concerns and trust constantly that our Bridegroom is taking the best care of us? Oh, yes, I trust in Your love for me and for all of my loved ones. I place them all in Your loving care. Please take care of each of them in Your own loving way—a way that sometimes seems so dark and mysterious to us. Oh Lord, if I trust in Your love, I will not spend one moment in worry. Instead, I will place all my cares in Your loving hands, knowing and trusting that You love me so much You will care for all my loved ones, be they family or friends.

> #92. "Let Christ crucified be enough for you, and with him suffer and take your rest, and hence annihilate yourself in all inward and outward things."

Upon reading this, I am overwhelmed with awe. Yes, Christ crucified is enough for me. I take my place in His suffering arms, and His outstretched hands. Why do I beg Him to take away my sufferings when I know they are His gift to me? I must learn to annihilate myself in all things, inward and outward. If I do this my life will become one solid prayer that I learn to suffer as Christ would have me suffer. I would learn to place all my sufferings into His wounded hands, to rest there on the Cross with Him.

When I first read this saying I was struck by the immensity of its' meaning...to annihilate ourselves...what a powerful saying...what deep meaning. It almost seems like we shouldn't love ourselves but that we should be happy only when we're suffering intensely. I don't think that's exactly what it means. Instead, I believe it means that we shouldn't always be striving for freedom from all suffering but that we should be ready for anything with great courage and fortitude. Instead of always choosing to be first, to be in the foreground, we should choose to be last, to be forgotten, to be drowned in the presence of God at all times and especially in moments of danger and hardship.

#93. "Endeavor always that things be not for you nor you for them, but forgetful of all, abide in recollection with your Bridegroom."

If only I could learn to do just that—to be forgetful of all, all the little worries and heartaches, and to abide constantly in recollection of Jesus, my Bridegroom. If I could only do that, I would never resort to worry and fear, and would understand that nothing matters except that I do everything for Him, with Him, in Him, with a heart filled with love for Him alone.

#94. "Have great love for trials and think of them as but a small way of pleasing your bridegroom, who did not hesitate to die for you."

Oh, how true that is—that Christ did not hesitate to die for me and for all,...to die a most hideous and cruel death. How much He must love each of us, for He would have died if we had been the only one on earth. That is how much He loves each of us. And so I think of trials as my small way of following in His footsteps, of living the Cross in daily life to the best of my ability, realizing that no matter how much I suffer, God will not let me suffer more than I can possibly suffer, and that if I unite all of my sufferings to His Cross on Calvary, I will gain an everlasting reward in heaven for all eternity.

#95. "Bear fortitude in your heart against all things that move you to that which is not God, and be a friend of the Passion of Christ."

I must strive very hard not to be moved by that which is not God, such as material wealth, more friends, success in my ventures, etc. All I really want, Dear Lord, is to be Your friend, a friend of Your Passion. This means that I seek to suffer with You and in You. I give You all my joys and successes, and ask for nothing in return except to love You more. So many things in life tempt me, but I see that they are not of You and so I should deny myself in this regard. I should not be swayed by compliments, nor should I accept Your gifts without the deepest humility and gratitude. How can I be a friend of Your Passion? By accepting willingly and lovingly all the little and big trials that life sends my way, I can be a friend of Your Passion. If they hurt me deeply, I should recognize that by accepting them lovingly I am joining in Your Passion. Oh Lord, please let me suffer with You and in You, now and forever, until I meet You in glory and suffer no more.

#96. "Be interiorly detached from all things and do not seek pleasure in any temporal thing, and your soul will concentrate on goods you do not know."

Oh Lord, please help me to learn detachment from all things. Help me to not seek pleasure in any temporal thing, but when I am gifted with pleasure, direct my thoughts immediately to You in thanksgiving and praise. You seem to spoil me, Lord, with Your many gifts and delights. I am so undeserving and I do not know how to properly thank You. Please help me to not seek pleasure apart from You and to concentrate on spiritual things, with the knowledge that they are the only things that really matter in this life.

#97. "The soul that walks in love neither tires others nor grows tired."

Dear Lord, I can't say enough about Your saying. I do walk in love, constantly, at every turn in life. I am constantly amazed at the pleasure You give to me in my walks of life. Everywhere I turn, in every task I undertake, You are there to lead me and guide me and reward me. I am overwhelmed by Your love. I can't begin to tell You how grateful I am for all that You do for me,...for all of Your marvelous gifts!

If I continue to walk in Your love, my life will go smoothly no matter what trial I have to face. I will always be happy if I continually walk with my hand in Yours. How can anything begin to dismay me if I never forget that You are close by, walking with me at all times?

#100. "The Father spoke one Word, which was His Son, and this Word he speaks always in eternal silence, and in silence must it be heard by the soul."

Silence is an important virtue. If we are to hear the Lord speak in our soul, we must give Him a chance. If we are always talking, or always busy, we will not have a chance to hear what Our Lord has to say to us. I live alone, and so I have plenty of silent time, but even then, I can keep so busy that I shut God out and have no room in my day for Him. I try very hard to fill most of my time with thoughts of God, or to have spiritual music in the background to help me be recollected. I try to fill my time with meaningful tasks during which time I can be recollected. Unlike many, I don't turn my TV on very much, and then when I do, I watch only programs

I feel God would approve of. Unfortunately, there aren't many TV programs which pass this test. And so, I spend most of my days and nights in relative silence.

#102. "He who seeks not the cross of Christ seeks not the glory of Christ."

Do I seek the cross of Christ? That is a huge question, and I'm not sure if I can answer it positively. I'm afraid that I seek after good health, and do everything necessary to preserve my health. However, the cross comes in many forms. I see the cross as affecting the lives of those whom I love, and try to encourage them. I don't know what crosses lie before me, but because of my age, I'm sure it won't be long before I'm asked to suffer. I pray fervently that I will willingly accept any suffering that comes my way and that I will not only accept it, but also will cherish it as a way of showing my love for God. Yes, I seek the glory of Christ, but I realize that this comes with the cross, and then, only if I accept it willingly and offer it to Christ as my gift of love for Him.

#103. "To be taken with love for a soul, God does not look on its greatness, but on the greatness of its humility."

Because this is true, I need not strive to be great in this life, but must strive, in everything, to be humble. If I am praised for anything, let me attribute it to God and His gifts. Without God's grace and His gifts, I would be a "nothing". And so, I try to utilize His gifts to the maximum, but I don't seek praise as though my gifts came from myself. No, any gift I possess comes from the hand of God. Because of this, it is important that I utilize all of my gifts to the best of my ability, and that I renounce praise but instead refer the praise to God, Who in His generosity gave me the gifts.

> #105. "Frequent combing gives the hair more luster and makes it easier to comb; a soul that frequently examines its thoughts, words and deeds, which are its hair, doing all things for the love of God, will have lustrous hair. Then the Bridegroom will look on the neck of the bride and thereby be captivated; and will be wounded by one of her eyes, that is, by the purity of intention she has in all she does. If in combing hair one wants it to have luster, one begins from the crown. All our works must begin from the crown (the love of God) if we wish them to be pure and lustrous."

This is so important to remember—that all our works must begin from the love of God if we wish them to be pure and lustrous…if we wish God to accept them from our lowly hands. With this thought in mind, I realize that everything I do each day, from getting up in the morning to going to bed at night, must be done with love for God. This is the only way that my gifts to God will be worth anything. With this in mind, I make a great effort to be mindful of God at every moment, and to continually offer all I do for His intentions. If I could do that consistently, I would probably very quickly become a saint.

> #108. "All the goodness we possess is lent to us, and God considers it his own work. God and his work is God."

We must always remember that any and all goodness we possess is lent to us, and God considers it His own work.

Sometimes, when I do a good deed, I get puffed up and carried away by praise, or by thinking I'm this great and wonderful person. No, I must realize that it is only through God and His grace that I can do anything good at all. Any good I do reflects the God that is within me. All I do I must do with this thought in mind—that I'm only doing God's will for me, and only this with the power of His grace. Therefore, I attribute all of my good actions to the wonderful grace of God in my soul, which comes from staying near to Him through the sacraments, and through constant awareness of His life in my soul.

> #109. "Wisdom enters through love, silence and mortification. It is great wisdom to know how to be silent and to look at neither the remarks, nor the deeds, nor the lives of others."

Not many people believe in the worth of silence and mortification. I do. I believe love is the most important of all virtues, but I also believe that there should be a place for silence and mortification in each of our days. During my day I make time for prayer and prayer can only take place in silence. Actually, I try to make my entire day one long prayer, but then there is a time when I sit down and pray to my hearts' content, and I can only do this in silence. I also believe in the worth of mortification. I look on mortification as another prayer. I offer it to God with the hope that He will accept it as a prayer for my most desperate needs. I find in my life that mortification is a necessary part of my day, and also believe that God sees and understands and answers all of my prayer requests, sometimes right away, but most often in His time which is not always the same as "my" time. I'm very confident that Our Lord sees and accepts all of my attempts at mortification.

I also believe that we should not look at the remarks, nor the deeds, nor the lives of others. Sometimes I find this to be nearly impossible, until I remember these words of St. John of the Cross. Then I look at my conscience, and try to clear it of all judgment. I live my own life as well as I can and try hard never to judge others. Among my friends and family, I see them living a variety of ways. There are those who are like me, and live entirely with heaven in mind, and there are those who are more worldly than I and maybe never give a thought to the final days or to eternity. All I can do is pray that everyone I love thinks more about eternity and the truth that all of our actions should be done with eternal life in mind as our goal.

> #112. "Allow yourself to be taught, allow yourself to receive orders, allow yourself to be subjected and despised, and you will be perfect."

Whenever I find myself subjected and despised, either by an acquaintance or a loved one, I come home and open my book to this saying, and I am deeply comforted. I realize that I must become more humble in order to accept this treatment without too much pain. I believe in the end it all comes down to humility. Do I have the humility to suffer others to despise me, my ways, my thoughts, my dreams? And do I have enough strength of character to keep from suffering in these instances? St. John of the Cross says…"and you will be perfect". After all, perfection is my goal, and so I will listen to his words of encouragement.

> #114. "Perfection does not lie in the virtues that the soul knows it has, but in the virtues that our Lord sees in

it. This is a closed book; hence one has no reason for presumption, but must remain prostrate on the ground with respect to self."

Yes, perfection is an elusive quality. The more we think we are perfect, or even close to perfection, the more we are guilty of pride. St. John says we must remain prostrate on the ground with respect to perfection. We cannot allow ourselves to believe we are perfect or we will be guilty of presumption. It is true; we cannot be our own judge. All we can do is our best, which many times is nowhere near to perfection. We leave it up to the Merciful Heart of Jesus to judge us, having within our hearts a great trust in His mercy. The deeper our trust in His mercy, the safer we will be. Our Lord is a just judge, but not a harsh judge. He is all merciful. He sees deep within our souls. He sees that many times we are not capable of heroic virtue, but He realizes completely that we are trying our hardest—that we are doing the best we can—and so, we have no need to fear, but trust completely in the graciousness of God's mercy.

#115. "Love consists not in feeling great things but in having great detachment and in suffering for the Beloved."

Most of our thoughts about love are mistaken. We think that to love Our Lord, we must always feel completely drawn to Him—totally under His spell. This is not true. Our Lord has great understanding. He understands the difficulties of our lives, and doesn't hold it against us if we can't be always smiling and happy. Sometimes we are much closer to God when we are suffering the most. To have great detachment is not easy but I think what St. John of the Cross means is that we should free ourselves of all worldly attachments, and not allow ourselves to be judged by worldly standards. How many times do we hear that we should glory in the Cross? In this worldly environment, everything we hear is how to escape the Cross—to escape suffering. If we suffer greatly, people feel sorry for us. And yet, great suffering can become our greatest gift because it will draw us closer to God if we let it. The key to this dilemma is that when we suffer we must offer it all to God for love of Him.

> #118. "Ignoring the imperfections of others, preserving silence and a continual communion with God will eradicate great imperfections from the soul and make it the possessor of great virtues."

I must make a great effort to ignore the imperfections of those close to me...my family and friends. It becomes easier when I remember the words of Our Lord about not looking at the splinter in the eyes of another, but to first take the plank out of our own eye. I try my hardest to overlook imperfections in others and to never, ever judge another. I can only do this with God's help, as I am just this lowly person striving to do what is right. As for preserving silence, I do try hard to preserve silence during the day when I am alone. I will add that I fill my silence many times with beautiful music and consider that the music greatly enhances the silent times. As for a continual communion with God, I strive for this every day and feel that I can come closer to this continual communion with God by starting my days with attending Mass and receiving Holy Communion. I believe that this is my way of setting the stage for living a life of virtue.

#120. "If a soul has more patience in suffering and more forbearance in going without satisfaction, the sign is there of its being more proficient in virtue."

I have so little to suffer, and so I can't really say I have a lot of patience in suffering. Looking to the future, I can only hope that I will always be patient in any sufferings the Lord chooses to send me. As for having forbearance in going without satisfaction, I will always strive for that in my life. Right now I am very fortunate to have very little suffering in my life, and so I don't have to try hard to have this forbearance in going without satisfaction.

It is important to remember that we need patience in times of trial and suffering. If I am hit with a disease of some kind, naturally I will suffer greatly. I hope that I will remember these words—to have patience in my suffering and the strength to live my life without ease or satisfaction. I will try to offer all of my sufferings for the good of souls and I'll try very hard not to complain.

#121. "The traits of the solitary bird are five: first, it seeks the highest place; second, it withstands no company; third, it holds its beak in the air; fourth, it has no definite color; fifth, it sings sweetly. These traits must be possessed by the contemplative soul. It must rise above passing things, paying no more heed to them than if they did not exist. It must likewise be so fond of silence and solitude that it does not tolerate the company of another creature. It must hold its beak in the air of the Holy Spirit, responding to his inspirations, that by so doing it may become worthy of his company. It must have no definite color, desiring to do nothing definite other than the will of God. It must sing sweetly in the contemplation and love of its Bridegroom."

I don't think I am a contemplative, but I do have a contemplative soul. I do try to rise above passing things, paying no more heed to them than is possible. I am very fond of silence and solitude, although I do have tolerance for the company of another person. Usually I am happy to once again be alone. I do try to listen to the Holy Spirit and respond to its' inspirations. One difference in my life, and I believe this is due to listening to the Holy Spirit, is that I go to the hospital to give Communion to the Catholic patients. Not too long ago I would have been way too fearful to undertake such a task. I try to do nothing definite other than the will of God. I'm sure that someday I will indeed enjoy the gift of contemplation and love of my Bridegroom.

#124. "Oh, how sweet your presence will be to me, you who are the supreme good! I must draw near you in silence and uncover Your feet that You may be pleased to unite me to you in marriage, and I will not rest until I rejoice in your arms. Now I ask you, Lord, not to abandon me at any time in my recollection, for I am a squanderer of my soul."

This is a cry of extreme love for Christ, the supreme good. It is the ultimate goal of the soul, to uncover Our Lord's feet that He may be pleased to be united with me in marriage. Here we are talking about the heights of the spiritual life—our goal. Until we meet this goal, and rejoice in Our Lord's arms, we will not rest. Here St. John of the Cross is talking about the spiritual marriage, which is the supreme end and goal for which we are striving. We need not be dismayed if we don't reach these heights, for very few do. We ask Our Lord not to abandon us at any time, and I am reassured that as long as I strive to be ever nearer to Him, He will not abandon me. I will not rest until I am safe in His arms.

> #125. "Detached from exterior things, dispossessed of interior things, disappropriated of the things of God—neither will prosperity detain you nor adversity hinder you."

If I am totally detached of exterior things—in other words, if all my material things were to vanish, and I wouldn't cry or be disturbed at all, then if I lost prosperity—which is having much, both in material things and in the gifts of God—I wouldn't be bothered by the loss of things or of God. If adversity were to come upon me, and I would lose all my material possessions, and even further, if I were to lose my closeness to God, which would be utter adversity, I would simply and humbly wait quietly and patiently upon the Lord, trusting that in His time, I would regain it all back, and I wouldn't be alarmed or hindered in my spiritual life.

This is the story of Job. I would try hard to follow his example by not grumbling or complaining of my misfortune. At such times, when we cannot see our way out of suffering, or do not know what the future holds, it is necessary to have great patience and deep trust in God, that God will eventually, in His own time, help us come through this dark tunnel bravely and with great patience, trusting blindly in the goodness and love of God.

#126. "The devil fears a soul united to God as he does God himself."

We can be sure that if we are united to God to any degree, the devil fears us as much as he fears God. This is a very reassuring thought.

#127. "The purest suffering produces the purest understanding.

This is such a promising statement. If we suffer purely for the glory of God, and offer all our sufferings to Him, we will gain a very pure understanding of God. We will understand the meaning behind suffering and we will be led to accept all our sufferings with joy, knowing how close they bring us to the Lord.

#128. "The soul that desires God to surrender himself to it entirely must surrender itself entirely to him without keeping anything for himself."

This is a very powerful statement. How do we surrender ourselves entirely to God? Can we do this on our own? I don't believe that we can do this on our own power, but the fact that God asks this of us implies that He will provide all that is necessary to accomplish this. We must give ourselves totally to God and keep nothing back for ourselves. Each day there are many opportunities to give of our self. We may be called to help our family members, or our neighbor. If we respond to this call with our whole heart, there will not be much room left in the day for self-will. Each moment of the day we should turn to God and ask Him—what do You want of me? What

can I do to serve You? I will try to free myself of self-will at
every moment of the day and night. We surrender ourselves
slowly, in this way, until one day we find that our will is totally
immersed in the will of God. For some of us, this may take a
lifetime. For other generous souls, they may offer their entire
being into the hands of God to do with them what He wills. It
isn't always easy to continually do what God wills of us, and
yet, this is the only way to becoming a saint, which is what I
want with my whole heart and soul.

#129. "The soul that has reached the union of love does
not even experience the first motions of sin."

Oh how I long for that day to arrive when I do not even
experience the first motions of sin. I must travel far along
the spiritual path before I can even think of being that close
to God that I would not experience the first motion of sin. It
seems so far away—so far beyond my reach...and yet, I know
this is what God wants of me, and I trust that He will draw
me close unto Himself, until that day when I will arrive at this
state of soul.

#132. "What we need most in order to make progress
is to be silent before this great God with our appetite
and with our tongues, for the language He best hears is
silent love."

To be silent before this great God with our appetite and
with our tongues means that we should not harbor thoughts
of selfishness or of longing for things, or for relationships.
Instead, we should be satisfied with very little in regard to
possessions, and with the few friends Our Lord has sent our

way. I believe we should treat every little thing we own as a treasure given us by God, but we should always be willing to give this up if somehow it is taken away. The same thing holds true for friends. We must relish all of our friends and look upon them as a gift from God. Yet we should always be ready to relinquish any friendship if this is what God asks of us. The language God best hears is silent love. Oh, what a great gift is silence. It is only in deep silence and recollection that we can come to know our God.

#134. "More is gained in one hour from God's good things than in a whole lifetime from your own."

God's good things are there for the asking. His good things are not always what we would see as good. Many times His good things are sufferings and hardships, because it is these which draw us closer to Him. One hour spent in God's presence can change our entire life. I often sit and reflect on Gods' good things for an hour or more, and when I get up to go about my day, I feel fortified beyond measure. At this time I find myself wishing, oh so much, that everyone in the world could be aware of this great treasure, which is a nearness to God.

I especially recall my visits of Adoration before the Blessed Sacrament one hour each week. After spending this hour so close to my Beloved, I come away with such fire and deep love that I think I can change the world. I wonder if it is possible to remain this close to Our Lord in the midst of daily life.

#135. "Love to be unknown both by yourself and by others. Never look at the good or evil of others."

I share my past life with others so they can see that having a mental illness does not have to mean the end of your life. I also share my life through writing, so as to help others along the spiritual path. Other than that, I try to be unknown, especially in regards to the inner life of the Spirit which I lead. As for being unknown to myself, that is immensely important, so as to achieve some semblance of humility. I try very hard to never look at the good or evil of others. I welcome other souls into my life without trying to assess their degree of spirituality. I can't say I am always successful. I do often admire the virtue I see in others, and I try to overlook the failings of others, knowing that only God can see into the depths of their soul. It takes great effort, sometimes, to avoid looking at another and judging them, but I try my hardest and ask Gods' help.

#136. "Walk in solitude with God; act according to the just measure; hide the blessings of God."

I find this saying hard to follow. I want to shout out and tell the whole world of the blessings of God. There are certain blessings for me alone, and I realize God does not want me to share. But for the most part, I share everything I can, what I am led to share, as a way of giving thanks and praise to God for His generosity to me as poor and lowly as I am. Most of my life I walk in solitude with God. I spend my days glorying in His presence, spending my day in prayer and thanksgiving for all He has done for me and is doing for me.

#138. "It is seriously wrong to have more regard for Gods' blessings than for God Himself: prayer and detachment."

In my prayer life, I must strive for detachment from all the blessings of God. I must count them as nothing. Yes, I must strive for God alone and His presence in my life, rather than striving for His special gifts and blessings. If Our Lord does send gifts my way I must learn to be detached from them, seeking only God and not His gifts.

#139. "Look at that infinite knowledge and that hidden spirit. What peace, what love, what silence is in that divine bosom! How lofty the science God teaches there, which is what we call the anagogical acts that so enkindle the heart."

This is what I strive for in my lifetime…to have this peace, love, and silence within my bosom. This is all I care about in this life. I open my heart to God and ask Him to teach me, in the most interior regions of my soul, the science of love. When God teaches me something about Himself, something about the interior life, what peace and love I experience deep in my soul. I can truly say my heart is enkindled with love for God.

#140. "The secret of one's conscience is considerably harmed and damaged as often as its fruits are manifested to others, for then one receives as reward the fruit of fleeting fame."

It is so true—to try and keep the fruits of Gods' gifts to myself, for when I share anything with others, I experience not reward, but the fruit of fleeting fame. Some of the good things in life I receive as a reward from God are things meant for me alone. If I share them, they lose the quality which they possess. I am less of a person for having shared them. I believe some things should not be shared simply because they are between me and God.

#143. "Do not excuse yourself or refuse to be corrected by all; listen to every reproof with a serene countenance; think that God utters it."

It is a sign of great humility to accept reproof from others without trying to excuse oneself, and to maintain a serene countenance. If we accept such comments with humility by thinking it is actually God Who is criticizing us, we will be able to weather the storm with great peace. I do not think it easy to arrive at such a state of deep humility. For myself, I have a long way to go before I can achieve such deep peace in the face of harsh criticism.

#144. "Live as though only God and yourself were in this world, so that your heart may not be detained by anything human."

Oh my Lord, if only I could do this…live as though You and I were the only ones in this world. I do try to live in Your presence every minute, every hour of every day. I try hard not to allow worry about my loved ones, friends as well as family, preoccupy my thoughts. Whenever I succeed in thinking solely of You, I am so greatly comforted that nothing has meaning for me except You and my love for You. Yes, I truly love my friends and my family, but I don't let them get in the way of my love for You. Instead, I let my thoughts of them turn to prayer, and in this way, I end up with thoughts of You. I realize that any thought of You comes from You, and in this way I strive for humility, which allows me to see that without You and Your love, I am nothing. St. Teresa of Avila addresses this issue in the following words…" Cleanse my lips, my heart, my whole life of the untruths, the petty pride, and self-love that so easily, so persistently come between us. Fill my night with Your forgiveness, with that peace that is possible only for those who walk in Your truth."8

> #146. "Never allow yourself to pour out your heart, even though it be but for the space of a Creed."

People try to pry things out of me, things which I feel are between the two of us alone. Please give me the strength of soul to not pour out my heart to anyone but You. I believe this is so important, because Your favors are for me alone, and if I were to share them with the world, their impact would diminish greatly. I would already have my reward, rather than waiting for eternal life, where all that You give to me, to us, will be a rich reward.

> #147. "Never listen to talk about the weaknesses of others, and if someone complains of another, you can tell her humbly to say nothing of it to you."

Lord, please guard my lips, so that I never talk about the weaknesses of others. When someone tries to draw me into a conversation about another, lead me to immediately spot it, and to notice that I am being drawn into gossip. Oh Lord, there is nothing worse than this, and I do my utmost to prevent it when

I hear it. I try so hard to say only good things of others, and if there is nothing good to say, then I don't say anything at all.

Actually, this saying goes along with another which tells us to always look for the good in others and to realize that what we see may not be the same that God sees. If we are careful not to judge others, we will not be tempted to talk about another's weakness realizing that what we see may not be weakness at all in the eyes of God.

#149. "Let all find compassion in you."

I find myself filled with compassion, and I know this is a gift from You, oh Lord. I see You in the faces of the suffering and I do what little I can to help bring relief to those who are suffering. I have so little to give, but I give what I can, and when I feel this is so very little, I turn to prayer, for I believe everyone is my sister and my brother and that I should do what I can to help them.

Almost every day I get mail asking me to share with the poor, the homeless, those less fortunate than I. I realize I cannot give to everyone who asks, and so I choose two causes which seem to me to be the most desperate people of all. I only give what I can which is not very much, but I believe God smiles at me for the effort and for the love with which I give.

#151. "Let your speech be such that no one may be offended, and let it concern things that would not cause you regret were all to know of them."

I often experience the opportunity to carry out this saying of St. John of the Cross. One of the jobs I do is as a leader. There are many occasions when I have to interrupt a conversation and remind people that they should never talk about someone who isn't present to defend themselves. It is not an easy task, because I am usually met with disfavor, but in the end, I succeed in stopping any and all gossip.

#152. "Do not refuse anything you possess, even though you may need it."

There are many occasions in my life when I see someone in need, and feel God is asking me to come to their rescue. Often, it is just a matter of giving of my surplus, but sometimes it's a matter of giving away something which I not only use, but which I need. I think of the young man in the Gospel who asked Our Lord what more he could do to come into the Kingdom, and Jesus told him to sell everything he had and give it to the poor, and the young man went away sad, for he had many possessions. This parable teaches me to give, not only of my surplus, but of my need. One must have a generous and loving heart, because there are always those in need. We don't have to look far to see them and to become aware that we could share of our possessions with them even if that means we go without.

#153. "Be silent concerning what God may have given you, and recall that saying of the bride: *My secret for myself.* [Is. 24:16] "

If God has chosen to give you great or mystical gifts, it is important to realize that you must keep this secret to yourself. The reason for this is that if you share God's special gifts with others, this will no doubt lead to pride. There is nothing more to fear than pride, for pride is what led the bad angels to their fall. We must escape pride in all its' ways and forms. If God has chosen to give us a gift, any gift, we should be most grateful, but also most careful not to reveal it to the world.

#154. "Strive to preserve your heart in peace; let no event of this world disturb it; reflect that all must come to an end."

There are many events that take place in ones' life which could disturb it. It is so important that we live our life in peace, and do not become disturbed by anything that might or might not happen. Whenever we are aware of the fact that something is disturbing us, we should immediately look to God for help, for of ourselves we do not have the strength or the ability to refrain from worry and stress. If we see that we are helpless to control our thoughts, we should immediately turn to God for help and ask Him to remove these stressful thoughts and fears from our mind. We are so little, and so helpless, and in many instances are completely unable to remove these stressful thoughts from our minds. Only by turning to God will we be saved from fear and troubling thoughts. I find there is only one way to handle such a situation, and that is to give it all to God. As St. John of the Cross says—"Reflect that all must come to an end."

#155. "Take neither great nor little notice of who is with you or against you, and try always to please God. Ask him that his will be done in you. Love him intensely, as he deserves to be loved."

I try very hard not to notice what others think of me, whether they are with me or against me. The only way I can succeed in this attempt is to do everything for the love of God. By always trying to please God, other motives simply slide away. I don't fear what others think of me, nor do I care. The reason for this is that whatever I do, I do trying to please God. This means I must constantly be asking God, "What is Your will for me?" Many times His will for me is not something I would have chosen for myself, but because I love Him intensely and try to please Him in everything I do, I end up doing things I never would have dreamed of doing. For example, I never would have dreamed of writing a book at the age of 72. I would have laughed at the idea. But then, age is irrelevant. I can write at the age of 72 or at the age of 92 if that is what He asks of me, only because I know that whatever He asks of me He gives me the grace to do it. As for loving God intensely, I hope that everyone in my life does love Him intensely. I'm writing this book to share how I try to love Him intensely with the desire that those who read it will have a little better idea of how to love God as He deserves to be loved.

#156. "Twelve stars for reaching the highest perfection: love of God, love of neighbor, obedience, chastity, poverty, penance, humility, mortification, prayers, silence, peace."

I realize I must examine my life to make sure all of these virtues are part of it. I look at love for my neighbor and I see that I could send more money to the missions. Am I obedient to the Word of God in all I do? As for chastity, I have always tried to live a pure life, but during my bi-polar episode, I failed miserably. Now that I am well, and have been for many years, I try hard to be chaste and pure in all of my thoughts, words and deeds. I turn to the Blessed Mother for inspiration in this, my effort. For mortification I do try to mortify my senses in many ways. I do lead a life of prayer and enjoy silence in my home. This silence brings with it great peace. I can only experience peace if I obey God in everything.

I realize that to reach all these virtues in their most perfect state actually takes a lifetime. I have only begun the practice of virtue and realize that I must strive after these virtues with all of my strength—my inner strength—and that until death. Hopefully on my deathbed I will have the assurance that I have practiced at least some of them in my lifetime. When I see God face to face I can only hope that I will not shrink from His sight because I have behaved poorly in my life. Rather, I hope that at the end of my life I can be reassured that I have tried with all the strength possible to attain some or all of these virtues.

#157. "Never take others for your example in the tasks you have to perform, however holy they may be, for the devil will set their imperfections before you. But imitate Christ, who is supremely perfect and supremely holy, and you will never err."

I am in the process of learning this. For many years, I set others as my example to follow, thinking them to be very holy, but over time I was disillusioned and this upset me greatly. In time I learned that I cannot judge another, either for the good or for the bad, and that above all, I must imitate Christ, Who is all perfect and all holy. By doing this, I am free of error.

#158. "Seek in reading and you will find in meditation; knock in prayer and it will be opened to you in contemplation."

I read spiritual books all the time, and this does lead me to meditate deeply on the mysteries of God. I pray every day as well, and leave myself open to the possibility that this will someday lead me into the prayer of contemplation, which is pure "gift" from God. I open myself to receive whatever gifts Our Lord chooses to send to me. I have strong faith that someday God will choose to grant me this most longed-for gift, and I realize it is a gift which I cannot earn, as much as I strive for it.

#159. "The further you withdraw from earthly things the closer you approach heavenly things and the more you find in God."

How I long to do this—to withdraw from earthly things. This is the only way I will become closer to heavenly things, and the more I will learn about God and approach God. Each day I believe I come a little closer to realizing this, as each day I deny myself earthly pleasures. I love it when people visit me, but for the most part, I spend my days alone. Even so, I never am alone, for I feel that God is very present in my small apartment. I feel that each day I am drawn closer and closer to God.

I notice that when I am able to forget about earthly things it is so much easier to concentrate on the things of God. On the contrary, when I am taken up with material things I lose some of that closeness to God. It is at these times that I am filled with sorrow, for closeness to God brings with it a great deal of happiness and peace.

#160. "Whoever knows how to die in all will have life in all."

To die in all—what a powerful statement! As much as I would like to die in all, there is still a part of me which clings to worldly enjoyment, and to worldly things. Some of these things I believe God has given me for my enjoyment, such as my gift of art or my gift of writing. It is because of these gifts that I have an outlet to serve others, and find this brings great enjoyment, which I believe is Gods' gift to me.

#163. The humble are those who hide in their own nothingness and know how to abandon themselves to God."

The humble hide in their own nothingness...they know that without Gods' help at every step, they can do nothing and are worth nothing. It is God's presence within them that gives meaning to their lives, and allows them to hold their head up high. They realize that any and all of their talents and abilities come from God as pure gift, and they do not become proud if and when people admire them, realizing that any and all of their "gift" is a pure gift from God, and that it is to be used for the honor and glory of God, rather than for their honor and glory. The humble person knows how to abandon themselves to God. He or she realizes that they are Gods', and that without God, they are nothing. Everything they do or say is for Gods' greater glory rather than for their own. If they have gifts to share with the world, they do not take credit for themselves, but give all the credit to God, the One Who gave them this gift. Through this understanding, they never grow proud of their accomplishments, but rather give all the praise and glory to God Who made them and Who gave them their gifts.

#164. "The meek are those who know how to suffer their neighbor and themselves."

Those who are meek never try to rise up in importance, but always try to remain unknown. If they have gifts or talents, they use these gifts for the greater honor and glory of God, never revelling in their great abundance, never wanting to be known by the world or to be praised as if the gift belonged to them. The meek will see others in the light of God. If they see the suffering, they see the face of God in the suffering. If they have wealth, their only thought is to share that wealth with the poor and needy and helpless. They do not attribute to themselves any claim to the gifts God has given them, but have only one aim in life, and that is to share their gifts by helping those who are in desperate need of help.

#165. "If you desire to be perfect, sell your will, give it to the poor in spirit, come to Christ in meekness and humility, and follow him to Calvary and the sepulcher."

This is the way of life as pointed out to us by St. John of the Cross. It is not going to be an easy path to follow. Many will be like the young rich man in the Gospels, who went away sad because he had many possessions. If I were rich, I would probably find it hard to follow Christ, but I am not rich. Yet, in comparison to the poor in many poverty stricken countries I am wealthy, and I realize it is important for me to give what

I am able to those who are in desperate need, for I see the face of Christ in the faces of the suffering, and I realize that I am not in want, but that all my basic needs are met. And so, I strive to give what I can, without suffering too much, realizing that even if I were to give more, I would not suffer, but would always have enough to eat and clothes on my back. I look at my life, and wonder what more can I do? There is always more that I can do. If I come to Christ in meekness and humility, I will always be searching for new ways of following Him to Calvary, and the sepulcher. God doesn't ask us to starve ourselves, or to give away what we need in order to live our life, but He does ask us to give until it hurts. He does ask us to open our eyes and see a world out there of people who are totally neglected, poor, hungry, and suffering. If we open our eyes to see this suffering, then we will not be able to go to bed well-fed and well-clothed without a thought for the poor children of God, who are all other Christs.

#166. "Those who trust in themselves are worse than the devil."

This is a hard saying and difficult to understand. In therapy, I have always been advised to trust in myself. And yet, here St. John is saying it is a bad thing. I think that is because he is so far beyond any of us in his spiritual life, and for him, he means to put all his trust in God and have little esteem for himself. This is the way of all the saints. With their deep humility, they see themselves as utter nothings, and rely totally on God for everything. Oh that I would someday come to that point. For now, all I can do is try to imitate St. Joh, to trust not in myself but completely in God.

#167. "Those who do not love their neighbor, abhor God."

Who is our neighbor? It is all people, rich or poor, friendly or unfriendly. I must love those who have hurt me, those who have abandoned me, those who suffer so terribly from hunger and thirst, from persecution and threat of starvation. If I love all people, I will find it in my heart to reach out to others in any way I can. It will be important for me to see the good in others and to act upon my inclination to help others, be they rich or poor. Many people who are rich are in greater need than I am, and it is important for me to see through the façade, to understand their needs and longings. Often I feel so greatly blessed, and it is with those blessing that I reach out to help others. As for material wealth, I have very little to give away, but when it comes to spiritual wealth, God has blessed me abundantly, and because of this I reach out to God for others' pain and spiritual need, and ask God to bless them.

#168. "Anyone who does things lukewarmly is close to falling."

I remember Our Lord saying something very negative about the lukewarm soul—that He will spit him out of His mouth. Yes, to be lukewarm is to lack the energy and commitment needed to become a saint—and we're all called to be a saint. Everyone must strive towards this goal with every ounce of their being. They should take on tasks that require great effort and not complain. To take the easy way out in every situation is to be lukewarm. To strive for perfection in all they do and in all they are asked to do—this is far from being lukewarm.

#169. "Whoever flees prayer flees all that is good."

A good part of my mornings are devoted to prayer. Without this, my life would be very empty. To flee prayer is to be unaware of our calling by God. Sometimes our prayer can be difficult and dry, and it seems no amount of effort on our part can make it good. That is probably a time when God is calling us to deeper prayer, possibly even to the prayer of contemplation. Many times I pray without any great feeling or satisfaction. Even during those times, I must persist and not give in to my feelings, for the spiritual writers tell us that in these times of darkness, we may be closer to God than ever before.

I try to make my whole life a prayer. When I am walking it is especially easy to pray for I am surrounded by God's beauty—the beauty of the trees or flowers or sky. The sky to me seems to be God's work of art, constantly changing, always different than any I have seen before, colors so unusual and awesome and so unbelievably breathtaking. I never tire of looking at the sky and "seeing" the Divine artist at work. Listening to beautiful music is also a time of prayer for me. I believe heaven will be filled with music and to hear its' beauty here on earth is for me a glimpse of heaven.

#170. "Conquering the tongue is better than fasting on bread and water."

Oh, how much damage we can do with our tongues. It is so important to watch what we say. I believe in a rule which says I never talk about another person unless I am saying something good. I try never to engage in gossip of any kind, and when

I hear it, I always try to stop it as tactfully as possible. I also have a rule for myself that I won't tell a lie to save the world. By this, I mean I will never never say anything but the truth. Having a rule like this firmly in my mind saves me a lot of trouble and I believe is very pleasing to God.

> #171. "Suffering for God is better than working miracles."

We are all called on to suffer at some time in our life. To consider suffering as better than working miracles gives us some idea of the value of suffering. Looking at it from a distance, it is easy for us to say yes, this is true. But when we are in the throes of suffering, it is not that easy to realize its' merit. I believe it makes suffering a lot easier to look at it this way—to realize that we can turn any and all suffering into a prayer. I offer my sufferings as a prayer to help other people, or to help those poor souls in purgatory. I see suffering as a great gift, especially when I come to realize how valuable it is. When I am given something to suffer, I look at it as a valuable cross which I can offer to God as a prayer—a very meaningful and valuable prayer.

> #172. Oh, what blessings we will enjoy in the vision of the Most Blessed Trinity!"

There are no words to describe the beauty and splendor of the Most Blessed Trinity! It takes faith to believe that this vision will one day be ours if we are faithful to God in both big and little things here on earth. It takes great faith to believe that one day, after living a virtuous life, we will go to heaven, where we will be blessed to see the Most Holy Trinity. Once we have arrived, we will realize that all our troubles here on earth amount to nothing in comparison to this, our great reward.

The Blessed Trinity is, of course, a great mystery which demands much faith in us. Faith is believing in something we can't see or understand. I believe that the mystery of the Blessed Trinity is one of the deepest and darkest mysteries we will be asked to believe in. Only in heaven will most of us come to see and understand this great mystery. I long for the day when God will enrich my mind with the understanding of this and all mysteries of faith.

173. "Do not be suspicious of your brother, for you will lose purity of heart."

I must keep this thought close to my heart, for I see that often times I tend to judge another. Because of this, I find myself greatly lacking in virtue. I must try to look at everyone as God would have me do—with great kindness and mercy, just as God looks at me and at everyone. Somehow I must come to imitate the Great and Merciful Heart of Jesus.

I believe that when we tend to be suspicious of another, we should acknowledge the fact that only God can read his or her heart and that we should not even attempt to understand what lies in the heart of another human being. We should try to be like God, looking at everyone with mercy even though we don't understand what motivates them or what lies beneath the actions they perform or the words they say. Let us be content, knowing that in heaven the doors of their hearts will be open to us. Here on earth we should realize that these mysteries will one day be revealed to us, but not now—only later—in heaven.

#174. "As for trials, the more the better."

Most of us shudder at the thought of coming trials—a diagnosis of disease, an untimely death in the family, a friend who betrays us, debt that has to be paid before we're ready, and on and on. How could it be possible for us to think like St. John of the Cross—the more trials, the better? We can only put on this mindset if we are very close to Our Lord. Then we will see that nothing happens that is not Gods' will. We ask ourselves, why does Our Lord will for me this tragedy, this trial? Most often, it is because Our Lord wants to draw us closer to Him. He wants us to rely more heavily upon His care and to trust more fully in His love. None of us knows what is around the bend for us. If we think along these lines, that the more trials the better, we will not face the future with fear and dread but with peace and serenity. We will have a strong enough faith to be able to place ourselves and our trials in the hands of a loving Father with great peace and serenity. We know God loves us more than we could ever imagine. Why, then, do we not trust this Father to allow what is best for us during our lifetime? It is always possible, with this trust in God, to face whatever trials life holds for us, and to live in great happiness, with much trust and great joy.

Whenever I experience trials, I open up my book and read this phrase. It brings peace to my heart to know there is something good to be said for trials. I then sit down and think over what could possibly be good about it. It strikes me that usually trials, in the end, make a better person of me. They give me more courage and stamina to go ahead and live the best I can amidst all of these trials, and when the end does come, I feel that I have indeed become a better person—a little wiser, a little stronger, a little more caring and loving.

#175. "What does anyone know who doesn't know how to suffer for Christ?"

This is indeed the crucial question. We all suffer at some time in our life. If we know how to suffer with grace, and even with generosity and joy, we will end up a much better person. I look at suffering as partaking in the sufferings of Christ. When I see how tremendously Our Lord suffered for us, by His choice, I understand that good can come from suffering if only we suffer in union with Christ by offering all our sufferings as a prayer to Him and in union with His suffering on the cross. He has chosen the cross as a means of redemption. Let us, then, choose the cross as a means of gaining our own redemption.

When I look at a crucifix, I immediately think of suffering. I can't help but wonder at the fact that the cross is venerated around the world. I ask the question—why? Why is Christ so closely related to the cross? Why did He choose suffering as the means of redemption? What does this tell us about our own suffering? Yes, I have a lot of questions, and only one answer. Christ's cross is a sign of His love for us. He chose suffering over every other possible way to redeem us. This says something about my cross, as yes, we each have a cross at some time during our life. Most of us would do anything to avoid suffering—to avoid the cross. I believe that anyone who wants to come close to Christ will choose to accept the cross with all that they are worth. They will see that by accepting suffering, and offering up this suffering as a prayer to help others, they are actually uniting themselves with Christ. They realize that the cross can be their vehicle on the road to heaven. They learn to love and respect the cross, whatever it may be. They, we, learn to love the cross as a medium of exchange—we exchange the cross as a key to opening heaven's gate.

MY GREATEST GIFT

Whom do I love above all?
It is You, my Dove.
You are my everything…
My desire, my gift, my Lover.

What do You ask of me?
That I give You all I own…
My goods, my desires, my hopes.
All this, and even more.

Can I ever give You enough?
No, never during my life…
Never can I give You enough
For all I have is from You.

What do I have that is not from You?
My family, my friends, my life…
You have given me more than I need,
More than I could ever wish for.

Above all, what gift is greatest?
Your Cross, Dear Lord, is my treasure…
Never will I complain of it,
That it is more than I can bear.

Is Your Cross my everything?
Yes, no matter how hard it seems…
I will cherish it close to my heart.
Every beat, I give it all to You.

How long will I sustain it?
As long as I live and breathe…
For my life is worth nothing without it.
It is truly my greatest treasure.

Why do I call it such?
Because it joins me closely to You…
If I offer it freely, generously,
I will never have reason to despair.

Is the Cross my answer?
Yes, it is that which I cherish most…
For it brings me face to face
With Someone Who suffered far more.

When will I see Your face Lord
So that I can identify with it?
As long as I trudge onward
My hand held tightly in Yours.

Is this all I ask of You?
Yes, that You allow me to cling
Closely to Yours, alone, in pain,
Until the end of my life.

Oh Lord, what a mystery You are!
The Cross leads to greatest joy…
To greatest happiness in this life
And to ecstasy in the next.

Dianne Marie Lotter, OCDS
December 25, 2011

SOMEONE SPECIAL

Why is my heart nearly breaking?
What is it causes such pain?
Must ungodly sensations stir me to the depths,
So that the abyss of feeling is in vain...
Beckons me taste once more the horrors of hell—for that's
what it nearly is?
I would rather fall into the vast immensity of the universe—
Floating forever through space—numb with terror and
despair—
Than to bear what I now bear.

Poetry cannot begin to penetrate the expression of this pain.
Perhaps music comes close.
The cadence, the flow of serenity following chaos—chaos
following serenity.
The contrasts, the rhythmic pulsation of something heard only
with the heart.
Yes, music begins to express—to capture the explosions of it.
It lulls me into numb forgetfulness—then,
Suddenly it tears into the reality of it.
It evokes the name of it—and if pain is something we can
name,
Well, then, that is a beginning to bearing it,
A step closer to unifying, offering, accepting it.

I need it all.
I need the poetry, I need the music, and I need the pain
As I fall through space—floating free—
Plunging despairingly, sensing now and then that

Someone special has me all along in a position quite
   precarious—
But now I have the perspicacity to see
It is He—He has given this to me.
And it really isn't precarious at all—it is Love. Only Love.

Dianne Marie Lotter 1985

Bibliography

The "Sayings of Light and Love" taken from *The Collected Works of St. John of the Cross* translated by Kieran Kavanaugh OCD and Otilio Rodreguez OCD.

1. Christian Prayer—Catholic Book Publishing Co. Page unknown.

2. Psalm 42—Christian Prayer—Catholic Book Publishing Co., p.793

3. Psalm 43—Christian Prayer—Catholic Book Publishing Co., p. 803

4. St. John of the Cross—"Light for the Journey"—Reflections from Carmel

5. "Living in the Presence of God" *Everyday Spirituality of Brother Lawrence* p. 169

6. "Noteworthy" *The Collected works of St. Teresa of Avila*

7. Elizabeth of the Trinitiy *"Praiseworthy"* Carmel of St. Joseph, p. 2

8. St. Teresa of Avila *"Light for the Journey"*—Reflections From Carmel

Would you like to see your manuscript become a book?

If you are interested in becoming a PublishAmerica author, please submit your manuscript for possible publication to us at:

acquisitions@publishamerica.com

You may also mail in your manuscript to:

**PublishAmerica
PO Box 151
Frederick, MD 21705**

We also offer free graphics for Children's Picture Books!

---

www.publishamerica.com

CPSIA information can be obtained at www.ICGtesting.com
Printed in the USA
LVOW082149070613

337575LV00001B/36/P